Central Sai...
...ry is for Aesthetic:
Essays on Creative and
Aesthetic Education

This was a Poet—It is That
Distils amazing sense
From ordinary Meanings—
An Attar so immense

From the familiar species
That perished by the Door—
We wonder it was not Ourselves
Arrested it—before—
                              Emily Dickinson

A is for Aesthetic: Essays on Creative and Aesthetic Education

Peter Abbs

The Falmer Press
(A member of the Taylor & Francis Group)
New York • Philadelphia • London

UK   The Falmer Press, Falmer House, Barcombe, Lewes,
      Sussex, BN8 5DL
USA   The Falmer Press, Taylor & Francis Inc., 242 Cherry St.
      Philadelphia, PA 19106 – 1906

First published 1989

Reprinted 1995

**Library of Congress Cataloguing-in-Publication Data
available on request**

British Library Cataloguing in Publication Data

Abbs, Peter
   A is for aesthetic: essays on creative
   and aesthetic education.
   1. Education.—Philosophical perspectives
   I. Title
   370′.1
   6 863288
   ISBN 1-85000-424-2
   ISBN 1-85000-425-0-Pbk

Jacket design by Caroline Archer

Cover illustration 'The Pilgrim Fool' (1942) reproduced
by kind permission of the artist Cecil Collins

*Printed in Great Britain by Burgess Science Press, Basingstoke
on paper which has a specified pH value on final paper
manufacture of not less than 7.5 and is therefore 'acid free'.*

Contents

List of Plates and Illustrations

General Acknowledgements

These essays, often in shorter versions and with different titles, have been given or published in the following places:

Chapter 1   *Creativity, The Arts and the Renewal of Culture* was given as the first *Louis Arnaud Reid Memorial Lecture* at the National Conference of Arts in Education, September 1986.

Chapter 2   *A Formal Aesthetic for the Teaching of the Arts* was the lead paper in *Creative and Aesthetic Education* published as *Aspects of Education No 34*, The Institute of Education, University of Hull, 1985.

Chapter 3   *English as an Arts Discipline* was first published as *Take up No. 2* for the National Association for Education in the Arts in 1985.

Chapter 4   *The Aesthetic Field of English* has been previously published in *Words*, January 1986.

Chapter 5   *Art and the Loss of Art in the Age of Spilt Science: The Demise of Late Modernism* was given at the Welsh Arts Council Annual Conference in August 1979.

Chapter 6   *Patterns to Which Growth May Aspire: The Place of Myth in Education*: an early version of this paper was first given at the Cockpit Theatre (London) Conference *Myth and Symbol* in March 1980 and published as the lead paper in *Tract 29/30*, 1980.

Chapter 7   *Education, Phantasy and the Inner Life of Feeling* was first given at the Kettering Foundation Conference on *Education and Values* at Woodstock, USA, June 1980 and subsequently published in *Teachers College Record*, New York, Spring 1981.

Chapter 8   *Education as Individuation: The Place of Autobiography* has developed out of an essay *Autobiography: Quest for Identity* published in *The New Pelican Guide to English Literature Volume 8*, 1983, edited by Boris Ford and an *Afterword* contributed to the *University of Sussex Occasional Paper No. 13 Autobiography and Education* edited by Trevor Pateman, 1986.

Chapter 9   *Towards a Conservationist Aesthetic* was originally commissioned as an advisory paper for the World Wildlife Fund in 1988.

Personal Acknowledgements

I would like to thank a number of people who have influenced the writing of this book. First I must thank all the students on the PGCE English and the MA Language, Arts and Education courses at the University of Sussex who over the last five years have been such a stimulus to my thinking. Next I must thank Professor Ernst Gombrich and Dr Trevor Pateman for reading and responding to some of the earlier drafts of some of the chapters. I must also thank David Bryce Smith for urging me to reflect on school architecture and for providing, at short notice, two of the photographs. Finally, I must thank my secretary Penny Searle, who has struggled to decipher my chaotic script, and my wife, who has constantly given both practical and emotional support as the idea of the book has gradually taken form. I am deeply indebted to all of them.

Introduction

If many of the authoritarian and utilitarian trends are to be effectively resisted, it is essential to have a better model of education, a model that is philosophically consistent, comprehensive in scope and historically grounded. It is hoped that these essays both formally presuppose and philosophically elaborate such a concept. The notion of education expounded in these pages has two major premises. The first is that *the proper methods of learning* are Socratic, dynamic and collaborative; the second is that *the balanced curriculum* should be built on a generic notion of human understanding. These, it is contested, are the key principles for the renewal of education; such a renewal depends not on standardized testing, not on mechanically linking knowledge to 'relevance', not on the *ad hoc* selection of ideologically favoured subjects, but rather, in the coordinated principles of dynamic learning and a plural epistemology.

The third aim of the book is connected to this notion of a plural epistemology. It is to offer a defence of the value of narrative, image, myth and phantasy (of what one might call the power of *imaginal and perceptual thinking*). They are among the primary means of symbolization and, hence, reflection and conception. Yet, after nursery and primary education they are as neglected by schools, colleges, and universities as they are cynically used and abused by the advertising industry. The three chapters of the book concentrating on phantasy, autobiography and myth are intended to dramatically reveal the way in which ethical and existential meaning can crystallize in these imaginal forms. They are also intended to demonstrate against the instrumental thinking of our time the interior and transformative nature of expressive educational activity.

Finally, and perhaps most crucially, following in the wake of *Living Powers* (Abbs, 1987), this volume seeks to reaffirm the indispensable place of the arts in any coherent curriculum. The arts (once freed from the narrowing restraints of an exhausted Modernism) represent one generic community of knowing, equal to while different from the other major symbolic communities: mathematics, the sciences and the humanities. While this notion has been formidably checked by the prescriptions of the proposed National Curriculum it is imperative that it is not lost – for, philosophically, it is an idea whose time has come.

It is hoped that these interrelated propositions, taken together and understood in the context of the specific arguments formulated in the pages that follow, advance that conservationist post-Modernist aesthetic now needed to combat the severe erosion of educational meaning in our society. Certainly it is with the joint purpose of *opposition* and *renewal* that these essays have been gathered together.

A is for Aesthetic and *Living Powers: the Arts in Education* are also intended to act as an intellectual prelude to a series of books on each of the major art disciplines and of their place in the school curriculum which Falmer Press will be publishing over the next few years.

Readers unfamiliar with the general argument of the book may find it valuable to read the last chapter first, for it offers a synoptic view of the conservationist aesthetic which informs the whole volume. Indeed, as the chapters have not been written consecutively (although their sequence has a certain logic) readers are invited to read the chapters in whatever order matches their own interests and inclinations.

Peter Abbs
University of Sussex
May 1988

Chapter 1
Creativity, the Arts and the Renewal of Culture

I must lie down where all the ladders start,
In the foul rag-and-bone shop of the heart.
W.B. Yeats

From the chuckle, the babble to the rhapsody.
Virginia Woolf

It is not possible to be original except on a basis of tradition.
D.W. Winnicott

Every art has the right to strike its roots in the art of a previous age.

Béla Bartók

Preamble

One of the terms essential to any understanding of education must be that of creativity. The word has come to denote a disposition of mind which is experimental, open, engaged, a particular kind of teaching and learning where the results cannot be comprehended in advance of the process, whether it be in mathematics, the sciences, the humanities or the arts. The word is indispensable in the vocabulary of all true education and, particularly, of aesthetic education. Isn't the educated mind the creative mind? I would want to answer in the affirmative, yet in the teaching of the arts there is a problem.

In the 1960s, under the broad influence of progressive educational theory and of Modernism, the word came to carry a number of associations which have made the case for an expressive and exploratory education infinitely more difficult to convincingly formulate for our own demanding time. During the 1960s the word became all but

1

synonymous with *originality*, with the subverting of conventions, with being different, with being individual, with 'doing one's own thing'. Virtually *any* act that broke with a norm was hailed as creative. *To be creative in the arts meant to be iconoclastic.* And yet this view distorted the deeper truths about creativity, namely that it would seem to be an inherent part of our common biological nature and that its full development requires a repertoire of received expressive forms, a living inheritance of examples and procedures transmitted by the culture. As it is in mathematics, the sciences and the humanities, so it is in the arts: one can only be significantly creative on the basis of tradition. Given a dynamic Socratic mode of teaching, *the better the tradition the better the chances of significant creativity*.

The current broad reaction against 'expressive' and 'open-ended' education can be understood partly as a reaction against the styles of teaching that developed out of the misplaced cult of originality with its belief in 'self-expression' and 'creativity'. We are paying a high price for that earlier Modernist iconoclasm of spirit. In response, our task as teachers and writers must be to conceptually reclaim rather than to reactively disown creativity; we must make the case for its existence in education more coherent, more comprehensive, more intellectually compelling.

The aim of this chapter is to delineate and interpret the creative process through whatever symbolic medium it may operate. In particular, I am keen to establish the connections and reciprocal continuities between nature and culture, between biology and symbol. It is also my belief that if we can formally understand the nature of the creative process we can begin to establish what kind of teaching best fosters it, what blunts and diminishes it. Thus at the end of the chapter I draw a number of conclusions about the implications of the argument for the teaching of the arts, which I then develop further in the following chapters.

Introduction

While creativity is, in its highest reaches, quite extraordinary, it is yet a common and everyday possession. Creativity, one might say, is the condition of our existence. It is not difficult to discern a creative energy at work in innumerable conversations, in sudden puns, spontaneous jokes, in the endless recreation of our experience into narrative form. It is not difficult to see it at work in children's play, and, of course, in infants' 'cuddlies' – those early transitional objects so precisely and lovingly described by the psychoanalyst D.W. Winnicott – in which inner emotional states and needs are given intimate symbolic form. The indispensable infant's rag is not merely a comforter, but basic material for the symbolic play of mind – for in the dawning psyche of the child the object comes to represent the absent mother. In this early symbolic leap of the psyche Winnicott saw the source of all cultural creation; in *Playing and Reality* he wrote: 'I have used the term cultural experience as an extension of the idea of transitional phenomena'[1] and claimed that in all acts of symbolic creativity he saw the same interplay between separateness and union.

And yet, of course, no understanding of creativity would be complete without an emphatic reference to *dreams*. And dreaming too is, in one sense, very ordinary. We all seem to have dreams without effort; it is a condition of our common existence. The dream involves, as we all know, the curious unwilled and unpredictable condensation of impulses into images, into montage, drama, story and surreal nonsense. Our liability to dream – our unconscious power to create imaginal narrative and iconic images – demonstrates a symbolic power at work in our biological nature. Indeed, the dream may offer one major clue to our more specialized notion of creativity as it manifests itself in the various artistic and scientific disciplines. The mode of the dream is imaginal and associative in structure, not discursive and rational, and it would seem that when the discursive and the rational has reached a kind of inevitable closure, the mind, if dynamic thinking is to continue, needs to step sideways and backwards into the more free, chaotic, seemingly crazy, open, suggestive modes of the dream-mentality. Most dreams offer a surreal logic – an uncanny logic of transformation through accident, suggestion and association – in which expected categories are broken down and new, often bizarre, relationships are formed. 'Dreamed of a wonderful pie made of blackberries, thrushes' eggs, honeycomb and watercress,'[2] wrote Hugh Walpole and in his dream we note the subversion of time worn categories and a further constellation of unexpected culinary relationships.

In other words, when we talk about creative activity we may be talking about *the transference of the night-time dream mentality to the day-time work of culture-making*. We could say that highly creative people are those who have elected the dream-mode as their *modus operandi*. They reclaim, and put to further use, those primitive modes of ideation which belong to the dynamics of the dream. They open themselves to the unconscious for their primary and potential material and then, through conscious

3

skill and labour, develop it into aesthetic and cultural form. To adapt the eloquent words of Dryden, the art-maker takes the sleeping images of things towards the light. As I shall show, such a view is very partial and incomplete – yet it does seem to carry a certain truth about much creative activity.

I have dived into creativity rather promptly, and gone deep! I want, though, in this chapter to establish the dream as one of the major clues to creativity. I want to suggest that one of the axes for understanding creativity is vertical. It concerns the continuous traffic, moving in both directions, upwards and downwards, between the conscious and the unconscious; or, more precisely, between the conscious, pre-conscious and unconscious. This would seem, at root, a primary biological dynamic: the conversion of impulse into image – and that may not be an adequate description of the process, for the image can seldom be understood solely in terms of the impulse. In the conversion a transformation takes place; and it is in that transformation that the power of cultural life lies. But, although this is one axis, there is another that is of equal importance. This is the axis that moves from innovation to tradition and from tradition back to innovation, a continuous, subtle, reciprocal movement between the received culture and the renewed culture. What I wish to establish is that which we call creativity – from the pun to the painting to the palindrome, from the cuddly-rag to rag-time to *Don Giovanni* – has to be comprehended and understood within the complex network set up by the four major terms: *conscious* and *unconscious, tradition* and *innovation*. That will be my major task in this essay, but first I must elaborate further the notion that creativity is not an esoteric power belonging only to a few exceptional individuals, but an innate power, part of our biological inheritance, part of what it is to be human.

A Historical and Philosophical Digression

Around the end of the eighteenth century there raged a profound argument about the nature of mind. On the one side were the Empiricists; on the other, the more metaphysical of the Romantics. The Empiricists claimed that the mind did not exist, as it were, until it encountered the objects of sense-perception and slowly through sensations it built up, block by block, its mental world. In their argument the Empiricists italicized *objects and things*, and from objects and things, by way of sense perception, derived all the furniture of the mind. The style in which they wrote was clipped, ordered, matter-of-fact, for they were presenting what they thought was mere common-sense. Thus Locke wrote in a famous passage:

> Let us then suppose the mind to be, as we say white paper, void of all characters, without any ideas: How comes it to be furnished? Whence comes it by that vast store which the busy and boundless fancy of man has painted on it with an almost endless variety? Whence has it all the materials of reason and knowledge? To this I answer, in one word, from Experience.[3]

Locke's 'one word' dispels with a clinical tap the multiplicity, efficiently dismisses, at a single blow, the busy and boundless fancy which *paints* an almost endless variety. (The verb is deeply significant; Locke had little place for the arts.) For Locke, like most English philosophers since, all knowledge derived from generalizations from experience, and experience derived from our knowledge of objects through sensations.

In English culture it was Coleridge, strongly influenced by his reading of German metaphysics, who was to dissent most passionately and tellingly from the Empiricist position. Coleridge, for example, wrote:

> Those who have been led to the same truths step by step, through the constant testimony of their senses, seem to me to want a sense which I possess. They contemplate nothing but parts, and all parts are necessarily little. And the universe to them is but a mass of little things. It is true, that the mind may become credulous and prone to superstition by the former method; but are not the experimentalists credulous even to madness in believing any absurdity, rather than believe the grandest truths, if they have not the testimony of their own senses in their favour? I have known some who have been rationally educated, as it is styled. They were marked by a microscopic acuteness, but when they looked at great things, all became a blank and they saw nothing, and denied (very illogically) that anything could be seen, and uniformly put the negation of a power for the possession of a power, and called the want of imagination judgment and the never being moved to rapture philosophy![4]

Coleridge sees totalities, sees patterns, sees connections which are not made through a kind of 'lego-building' in which a set number of blocks make a mental unit. The tree we see through vision is not the sum-total of leaves and branches. Coleridge, we would say in modern terms, is affirming the truth of *the gestalt*: the power we possess to see creatively, not in parts which sequentially build up into wholes, but immediately in totalities. I would say, rather rashly, that Coleridge emerges in our own century as the champion of that great philosophical contest. Biologists, psychologists, philosophers, linguists, literary critics now tend to assume – with Coleridge (and with Kant) – that the mind has to bring categories to experience in order to make sense of it. It would seem that there is an inherent disposition towards certain kinds of pattern-making in the structure of the mind. The child is not a *tabula rasa* at birth, as any mother knows – but a personality with a number of distinctive orientations towards order and meaning, human order, human meaning. The baby is an active agent. It does not move at random nor does it move like a robot, determined solely by the impinging dictates of the environment. It is guided unconsciously by an inbuilt sense of biologically inherited order: that sense of order, as Kant and Coleridge argued, is logically prior to the world it encounters and then collaborates with. The mother doesn't plant on her baby the idea of the transitional object nor does the child learn it from a sister or brother. It is, it would seem, a primary symbolic need of the child's nature. Likewise the child does not learn to dream. *The psyche dreams.* Of course, all of these symbol-making, shape-creating energies enter an actual culture – and are profoundly influenced by the conscious and unconscious content of that culture – but they cannot be causally derived from it. They are autonomous energies, biologically given.

The distinguished art-critic Ernst Gombrich has written, in a book significantly entitled *The Sense of Order*, that:

> There is an observable bias in our perception for simple configurations, straight lines, circles and other simple orders and we will tend to see such regularities rather than random shapes in our encounter with the chaotic world outside.[5]

Of course, the world outside may not be chaotic but subject to other regularities: what would seem philosophically most probable is that we always mediate that world through our categories. We can only know a human world, *a co-existence of consciousness and object* – a theme which I will return to in the last chapter. Science reveals as much about us as what it claims to describe. As the scientist J.Z. Young has written:

> In some sense we literally create the world we speak about. Therefore our physical science is not simply a set of reports

about an outside world. It is also a report about ourselves and our relations to that world, whatever the latter may be like.[6]

However, it is this innate power to 'literally create the world' (in some sense) which concerns us here, not the epistemological dilemmas it creates.

The Innateness of Creativity

One way of demonstrating this immediate creativity is, in the manner of the Gestalt school of psychology, to consider the following marks:

It is all but impossible *not* to see these marks as forming definitive configurations. We immediately see (*mediate* at once, that is) three dots as a triangle; four as a square; the broken lines as a triangle and the oval with three horizontal lines as a human face. We know, furthermore, in everyday life how we constantly complete the fractured syntax of passing posters, headlines, advertisements, the missing letters of key words. We invariably, symbolically and perceptually conclude the often inconclusive data of our serrated experience as it streams past and beyond us. But Gombrich in *The Sense of Order* was out to establish a larger point; not only that there are inherent aesthetic, perceptual and symbolic tendencies towards order, *but that there may be a kind of continuum from the simple to the complex, from the merely pleasing and instinctively gratifying to the intrinsically sublime.* With immense suggestiveness, he reproduces together 'the drawings' of Congo (the ape) and a drawing of Raphael (the Renaissance artist) and refers to 'rhythmical propensities of the organism which reach from the sub-human level of Congo's brushwork to the sublime feeling for rhythm and form which makes a master such as Raphael'. It is *this* connection, cutting through all the obvious differences between the two which, in this context of creativity, is so *resonant*. It is comparable to that connection Winnicott saw between the smelly piece of rag, so vital to the child, and the creation of cathedrals, epics, and scientific theories. There is a continuum in the creative art which moves from the ordinary to the extraordinary, from daily perceptual vision to deep analogical vision, to the rhythmic babblings and repetitions of pre-verbal utterance to the regular beat and syntactic echoing of epic and poetry. The forms of art are not arbitrarily invented; they proceed from the instinctual movements of the body and the interior shapes and dispositions of the inherited mind. As Barbara Hardy has said about the novel: 'the narratives of artistic fiction must be seen as a primary act of mind transferred to art from life'[7]: so it is with image, rhythm, movement – in fact, all the essential elements of aesthetic experience.

Our creativity is *natural*, the symbols it gives birth to are intricate and continuous elaborations of our intrinsic natures, not necessarily a distortion of the sexual urge (as Freud suggested), nor an epiphenomenon of the economic system (as Marx maintained) nor a distraction or leisure pursuit (as Thatcherites would have it). The creation and amplification of symbols is at once a primary need and a primitive endowment. The French Revolution gave three political imperatives: Liberty, Fraternity, Equality; but as great as these, and biologically much deeper, is the imperative of symbolic creation.

Plates 1 and 2   Drawings by Congo

Plate 3   Drawing of Virgin and Child *by Raphael circa 1505.*
With immense suggestiveness Ernst Gombrich links the drawings of Congo the ape (figures 1 and 2) with the drawing of Raphael and refers to those rhythmical propensities which reach from the sub-human to the sublime.

Humankind has a biological need to live in and contribute to a symbolically rich universe.

The Vertical Axis of Creativity

I want now to turn to the first axis of creativity, the movement between the conscious and the unconscious.

To illuminate the vertical axis of creativity, namely:

CONSCIOUS

↓ ↑

PRECONSCIOUS

↓ ↑

UNCONSCIOUS

it is necessary to consider more closely the phenomenon of the dream. I claimed earlier that one major clue to creativity may lie in the transference of the night-time dream modality to the day-time work of culture-making. In this transference the powerful unconscious patterning processes of the psyche-soma are used and elaborated in the creation of art, theory and science. Einstein answering a questionnaire[8] about creativity in 1945 claimed that 'combinatory play' was the essential feature of productive thinking. Combinatory play – allowing for a whole range of sequencing and connecting which can both use and break the established congruences, both convert and invert the settled narratives – is another way of describing the dream modality. Of its primitive nature, Einstein was aware: he called this kind of thinking 'visual' (as opposed to discursive) and 'muscular' (as opposed to intellectual). For creative thinking to happen one must constantly step *sideways* out of the track set by logic and *downwards* into the unconscious.

Einstein wrote in answer to the questionnaire:

> Conventional words or other signs have to be sought for laboriously only in a secondary stage, when the mentioned associative play is sufficiently established and can be reproduced at will.[9]

Here in Einstein's famous formulation it can be seen that creativity may involve a continuous movement between primary associative ideation and secondary conceptual elaboration inside a particular tradition and symbolic form. Neatly condensed, Einstein's remark reveals the dialectics of creativity, the movements between both the vertical and horizontal axes. But to understand this dialectic we need to move more carefully. We need to examine the vertical axis through the phenomenon of the dream.

We can probably all give personal examples of involuntary acts of mind in which objects in the world are recreated in new imaginal contexts in which simple events are taken from their habitual frames and placed in new frames and their content dramatically rearranged according to another set of principles. This is what the dream and dream-phenomena do. I want to take for my example a dream of a man called Herbert Silberer.

Susanne Langer in *Mind: An Essay on Human Feeling* records the dream of Herbert Silberer when he is riding in a European railroad coach. Silberer, describing the starting point of the dream, writes:

> With my eyes closed, I am leaning against the corner of the compartment. Time and again the setting sun shines into my face. It disturbs me but I am too tired to get up and draw the shade. So I let it shine on me and watch the visual impressions that come as the sunshine hits my eyelids. Remarkably enough, the figures are different each time, but each time uniform ... I see a mosaic of triangles, then one of squares and so on   Then I have the impression that I myself am putting together the mosaic figures in rhythmical movements. Soon I find that the rhythm is that of the axles of the train ... All of a sudden the following autosymbolic phenomenon occurs: I see an old lady, to the right, setting a table with a checkered table cloth, each square of which encloses a figure resembling one of the sun-mosaics previously mentioned, the figures are all different.[10]

The account records a steady movement from the conscious to the unconscious: from being aware of the visual impressions created by the sun, from being in a semi-conscious trance state in which he feels he is creating the mosaic effects, from, finally, sinking into sleep when the unconscious begins to recreate the phenomena in terms of narrative and character. In this account the actual sense-perception provides the immediate material for the dream imagination. By some spontaneous unconscious process, the bright sunshine is being further abstracted and recast in terms of a new matrix: an old lady is laying a table with a sun-mosaic tablecloth. The conscious hypnotic sense-perception is taking on symbolic form, is forming the material of another narrative and drama. Silberer calls his dream, as opposed to his trance, 'auto-symbolic phenomenon'. I want to suggest the sequence demonstrates the characteristic marks of the creative process: there is a playing with patterns, there is a shifting of reference from one matrix (that of ordinary perceptual experience) to another (that of symbol and narrative); there is the transformation of ordinary experience according to some inner need, categories and, possibly, archetypes. Why is the woman there? Why is she old? Why is she laying the sun-checkered table-cloth? Here is an example of creativity: *quite ordinary* and yet, on further reflection, *quite extraordinary*, performed without effort as the individual's consciousness drifted into the unconscious and its 'auto-symbolic phenomenon'.

Susanne Langer considering Silberer's dream claimed that:

> It is in dream that the imaginative powers are born and exercised without effort or intention, unfold, and finally possess all departments of sense, and activate another great class of largely uncomprehended phenomena, the products of memory. Remembered sights and sounds, often unrecorded in conscious experience, sometimes whole situations especially of early life, tactile and olfactory and muscular impressions come together to form the profuse unsolicited imagery our brains create in sleep.[11]

Dream, she suggests, creates the imaginative powers that are then extended to other conscious activities in the course of evolutionary development. This would explain why the first great mode of cultural thinking is mythic in nature, structured, that is to say, through deep personification, through narrative sequence and metaphor. Considering the functions of dream in the evolutionary shift from animal mentality to symbol-making mind, Langer wrote:

> The transition from the automatic completion of started acts which were curtailed in the mêlée of impulses seeking expression, to the deliberate envisagement of things not present and situations not actually given is another major move in the shift from animal mentality to mind ... Symbolism is the mark of humanity, and its evolution was probably slow and cumulative, until the characteristic mental function, semantic intuition – the perception of meaning – emerged from the unconscious process Freud called the dream-work into conscious experience.[12]

It is not possible or necessary to pursue here the evolutionary element in Langer's argument. What is essential to our case is the mode and manner of an inherent kind of creativity in the human psyche: the condensation of impulses into images and the conversion of images into material for conscious combinatory play and general culture-making.

We do not know whether Silberer's dream was emotionally or aesthetically moving or whether he felt moved to paint an image of it or represent it in some other artistic form. It is unlikely. And yet there are many examples of the development of auto-symbolic phenomenon into works of artistic greatness. The inspiration, for example, of Stravinsky's *The Rite of Spring* derived from a dream the composer had of a dancer dancing herself to death before a ring of priestly spectators; Michael Tippett's *The Midsummer Marriage* developed out of an active phantasy involving the goddess Athena and the god Dionysus, those 'magical archetypes'. He was later to write:

> even now some of the excitement of these first pictures come back. It is the feeling a creative artist has when he knows he has become the instrument of some collective imaginative experience – or, as Wagner put it, that a Myth is coming once more to life. [13]

Tippett's reference to Wagner recalls a further celebrated example of the unconscious not forming the initial inspiration but actually creating the form of the art. In the example the creative movement is from the conscious down to the unconscious and back to consciousness, with the dilemma resolved. This is Wagner's own account of the composition of the orchestral introduction to *Rheingold*:

> After a night spent in fever and sleeplessness, I forced myself to take a long tramp the next day through the hilly country, which was covered with pinewoods. It all looked dreary and desolate, and I could not think what I should do there. Returning in the afternoon, I stretched myself, dead tired, on a hard couch, awaiting the long-desired hour of sleep. It did not come; but I fell into a kind of somnolent state, in which I suddenly felt as though I were sinking in swiftly flowing water. The rushing sound formed itself in my brain into a musical sound, the chord of E flat major, which continually re-echoed in broken forms; these broken chords which seemed to be melodic passages of increasing motion, yet the pure triad of E flat major never changed, but seemed by its continuance to impart infinite significance to the element in which I was sinking. I awoke in sudden terror from my doze, feeling as though the waves were

rushing high above my head. I, at once, recognised that the orchestral overture to the *Rheingold*, which must long have lain latent within me though it had been unable to find definite form, had at last been revealed to me. I then quickly realised my own nature; the stream of life was not to flow to me from without, but from within. [14]

Wagner's artistic paralysis is broken in the somnolent state. In that state what was consciously hunted for rises spontaneously with the kinaesthetic sensation of water flowing. This may be a good example of Einstein's 'muscular thinking'. (Is it also possible that the terror relates to a dread of sinking too far into the plethora of the unconscious?) But, for our general argument, the phenomenon itself speaks clearly enough: 'the chord of E flat major ... continually re-echoed in broken forms' is heard, for the first time, in a state of dream-like trance.

There are many examples, both in the sciences and the arts, of such creative activity. In her introduction to *Frankenstein* Mary Shelley explained how in a dream trance, 'with shut eyes, but acute mental vision', she saw the pale student bringing 'the hideous phantasm of a man' to life and foresaw all its terrible narrative implications:

Swift as light and as cheering was the idea that broke in upon me. 'I have found it! What terrified me will terrify others; and I need only describe the spectre which had haunted my midnight pillow.' On the morrow I announced that I had thought of a story. [15]

R.L. Stevenson, in a similar manner, tells us how in a dream he was given the crucial episode in *Dr. Jekyll and Mr. Hyde*:

For two days I went about racking my brains for a plot of any sort; and on the second night I dreamed the scene at the window and a scene afterwards split in two, in which Hyde, pursued for some crime, took the powder and underwent the change in the presence of his pursuers. [16]

While Katherine Mansfield tells us in her *Letters and Journals* the origin of her short story *Sun and Moon*:

I dreamed a short story last night, even down to its name, which was *Sun and Moon*. It was very light. I dreamed it all – about children. I got up at 6.30 and wrote a note or two because I knew it would fade, I'll send it some time this week. It's so nice. I didn't dream that I read it. No, I was in it, part of it, and it played round invisible me. But the hero is not more than 5. In my dream I saw a supper table with the eyes of 5. It was awfully queer – especially a plate of half-melted ice-cream ...[17]

I have taken my examples from the arts but there are many examples of the same kind of creative process in the sciences. Indeed, it was an eminent scientist, Kekulé, who discovered through hallucinatory dream images the structure of benzine and concluded a famous lecture on science with the injunction: 'Let us dream, gentlemen.'[18]

Yet, as Kekulé himself knew, dreaming is not sufficient. What is necessary is *consciously* developing a dream-like disposition; a disposition which allows the mind to enter the associative labyrinth, the surreal city, the primordial underground. In order to be creative one must develop a disposition to doodle, to let the marks create the marks that the mind then dreamily follows. The following piece of free-association, automatic writing exemplifies the process. It is by Coleridge and is taken from one of his many note-books:

... I inevitably by some link or other return to you, or (say rather) bring some fuel of thought to the ceaseless Yearning for you at my Inmost, which like a steady fire attracts constantly the air which constantly feeds it) I began strictly and as matter of fact to examine that subtle Vulcanian Spider-web Net of Steel – strong as Steel yet subtle as the Ether, in which my soul flutters inclosed with the Idea of your's   to pass rapidly as in a catalogue thro' the Images only, exclusive of the thousand Thoughts that possess the same force, which never fail instantly to wake into vivider flame the for ever and ever Feeling of you/
   The fire/ – Mary, you, and I at Gallow-Hill/ – or if flamy, reflected in children's round faces   ah whose children? – a dog – that dog whose restless eyes oft catching the light of the fire used to watch your face, as you leaned with your head on your hand and arm, & your feet on the fender/the fender thence/ – Fowls at Table – the last dinner at Gallow Hill, when you drest the two fowls in that delicious white Sauce which when very ill is the only idea of food that does not make me sicker/all natural Scenery – ten thousand links, and if it please me, the very spasm & drawing-back of a pleasure which is half-pain, you not being there – Cheese – at Middleham, too salt/horses, my ride to Scarborough – asses, to that large living 2 or 3 miles from Middleham/All Books – my Study at Keswick/ – the Ceiling or Head of a Bed – the green watered Mazarine! – a Candle in its

socket, with its alternate fits & dying flashes of lingering Light
– O God! O God! – Books of abstruse Knowledge – the
Thomas Aquinas & Suarez from the Durham Library/ – a peony
faced cottage Girl – little Jane/all articles of female dress –
music – the opening of a Street door – when you first came to
Keswick – ... Letters, year, the very paper on which one might
be written – or from the habit of half unconsciously writing
your name or its Symbol invented by me to express it – all
Travels/my yearning Absence/all books of natural History –
...the Heavens/your name in those bright Stars, or an M or W
recalling those Stars – Aurora borealis – at Keswick by the
corner parlour window...[19]

In this hyphenated stream-of-consciousness writing Coleridge
passes, with dramatic rapidity, from image to image, following through
memory and association and suggestion their 'ten thousand links',
thereby creating a spider-web of intimate and poetic connections. This
is private incantatory writing: writing for both the direct exploration
and the immediate ease of a disturbed consciousness. It is not written
for an audience. It is not a poem. It is not an artefact which conforms to
any genre. Not yet: but, of course, it could have become so. It is the
primary polymorphic material of poetry; the auto-symbolic stuff of the
dream-mind tapped by the conscious mind and allowed to flow. Were
it to develop further, the next stage would be for Coleridge, *the poet*,
to select, to edit, to amplify, to shape into a tighter/poetic form the
half-random ramblings of his own mind. Indeed, a few of the lines seem
already to possess the intensity and precision of poetry: 'a candle in its
socket, with its socket, with its alternate fits and dying flashes of
lingering light': 'the very spasm and drawing back of a pleasure which
is half-pain': 'my soul flutters enclosed' ... These are semantic gifts from
the unconscious found by the writer using his pen as a kind of divining
rod to locate the subterranean elements below. They reveal what Arthur
Koestler in his study of creativity described as 'the momentary regress-
ions to earlier stages in mental evolution, bringing forms, of mentation
into play which otherwise manifest themselves only in the dream
or dream-like state'. They reveal a creative regression back into the
unconscious and into the dream modality. Coleridge knew exactly what
he was doing. In the margin's of Southey's *Life of Bunyan* Coleridge
wrote:

But the *Pen* is the Tongue of a systematic Dream – a Somnolo-
quist! ... During this state of continuous not single-mindedness,

but *one*-SIDE-mindedness. Writing is manual Somnambulism
– the somnial Magic superinduced on, without suspending, the
active powers of the mind.[20]

Essentially, what is manifest in many of Coleridge's journal entries
is a creative regression; and this movement between the conscious and
the unconscious which such a regression entails I have suggested forms
the vertical axis of the creative act. But the creative act invariably
involves, also, a creative elaboration in terms of the symbolic form
within which it operates. Physics involves a knowledge of physics,
music a knowledge of music, philosophy of philosophy. Wagner could
not only hear a certain sound, he could also *interpret* that sound *musically*
and *render* it *musically*, and musically, not just in general terms, but in
terms of evolving nineteenth-century Romantic traditions. Without
those traditions, without that historic context, the sound would not
have become the orchestral introduction to *Rheingold*. In fact, it is all but
impossible to conceive of Wagner's composition being written in an
earlier century; and its actual writing depended not on trance states, but
on skill, knowledge of the medium, and incessant labour. For highly
creative individuals are not only able to submit to the dream modality,
they are also able to construct and complete durable public works
which outlast the ephemera and inconsequentiality of the private and
culturally inaccessible dream.

This brings me to the other major axis of creativity: the horizontal
axis, that between tradition and innovation.

The Horizontal Axis of Creativity

I have claimed that the unconscious is a shaping energy, helping to
determine the form of creative work, but it is also true that, in a certain
manner of speaking, *symbolic forms create symbolic forms*, that art creates
art, that science creates science, that theory creates theory; that, in all
culture, there is a constant reworking of the established conventions,
notations, images, narratives; that, at nearly all times in the creation
of new art, new science and new theory there are constant acts of
plagiarism and theft, acts which are redeemed by the further adaptation
to which the stolen material is deftly put before it is stolen again and
cast, yet again, in another shape, always in part derivative, always in
part potentially new. Creativity, in brief, cannot be understood without
reference to the symbolic field in which it takes place – that complex

magnetic system of allusion, notation, reference, narrative, knowledge, assumption, understanding which we call culture and in their specific contexts the cultures of the various symbolic forms. It is precisely *this* dialectical relationship between inherited culture and symbolic transformation, between tradition and innovation, which marks the horizontal axis of creativity.

Consider a contemporary artist who would, on first response, appear to work directly from immediate sensation, without reference to a cultural past or to a series of tested conventions: Francis Bacon. Yet a closer look at his work, particularly his best, demonstrates the continuous recreation of tradition. Bacon's creativity is often working from and through the creative achievement of previous painters whose work is recast into new configurations, which still carry with them the memory of the tradition.

As the introduction to the catalogue[21] for the Tate Gallery *Francis Bacon* amply shows, the work of this seemingly atavistic and disinherited painter is profoundly indebted to Rembrandt, Poussin, Caravaggio, Velasquez, Ingres, Van Gogh and Picasso. For some of his images he is also indebted to the cinema of Eisenstein and the photographs of J.A. Boiffard and, in particular, Edward Muybridge; and beyond these a debt is recorded to T.S. Eliot, Nietzsche, Valèry, as also Aeschylus and the Greek myths. Hellenic and Hebraic memories of violence and hideous suffering run like a high-voltage electric current through his paintings. In the best of his savagely truncated work some of the key myths of our Greek and Christian culture are simultaneously repeated *and* transformed. It is this creative connection with the inherited forms which I am anxious to stress. The Modernism of Bacon is very ancient.

An early painting by Bacon – *Figure with Meat* (1954) – brings out well the debt to inherited images that go back and back from Picasso to Soutine to Goya, to Rembrandt into the innumerable crosses and crucifixes that mark the half-historic, half-mythic event of Christ's sacrifice. Powerful webs of association and feeling are connected in the collective mind to this historico-mythical event and each painting of a crucifixion draws on them all and is indebted to them all for whatever power it still carries. Rembrandt is able to tap that subterranean complex of feeling merely by painting a carcass at a particular angle and bathing it in an unnatural light – and this remarkable artistic achievement deepens and adds to the very energy it draws upon. *And Rembrandt (plate 4) makes the work of Soutine (plate 5) possible. And Soutine, the work of Bacon (plate 6).* Where then lies the creativity? From

Plate 4   Rembrandt The Slaughtered Ox
1655.

Plate 5   *Soutine* Carcass of Beef 1926

Plate 6   *Bacon* Painting 1946

19

this perspective it can only be located in the endless labour of transformation, in the movement backwards and forwards along the horizontal axis of tradition and innovation, of creation and recreation, of the received and the renewed.

We think of Shakespeare as prodigiously inventive – a genius of originality – yet he was also the master of all plagiarists, the best of the magpies, assembling the materials for his art from wherever he could find them. There is a story called *Amleth* written by Saxo. In this story we have a wicked uncle and a threatened nephew who plays the fool while seeking revenge; we have a girl to whom the hero is attracted but does not marry; we have the ruthless murder of a spy, bitter reproaches to a faithless mother, a voyage intended to end in the hero's death, his return home and the final achievement of his revenge in which many beside his uncle die. Amleth, in narrative terms, is the prototype of Hamlet. Only the ghost and the travelling players are missing from *Amleth*, and these, too, can be found in earlier tales by Saxo. Shakespeare simply lifts the story and puts it to further aesthetic and dramatic use.

In his *Conversations with Eckermann* Goethe wrote:

> People are always talking of originality but what does that mean? As soon as we are born the world begins to act on us and this goes on to the end. And, after all, what can we call our own, except energy, strength and will?
>
> If I could give an account of all I owe to great predecessors and contemporaries, there would be but a small balance in my favour ... I, by no means, owe my works to my wisdom alone, but to a thousand things and persons around me, that provided me with material.[22]

Originality, it would seem, can only have meaning in terms of the origin of the debt, adaptations and transformations made possible by the material of the received culture.

The horizontal axis yields a radically different perception into the creative process from that of the vertical. And yet they are not mutually exclusive but in intricate relationship, together forming the warp and the weft of active symbolic creation., If we return to consider some of our earlier examples of creativity (of Stravinsky, Tippett and Wagner) we can see that these gifts from the unconscious came to individuals who were highly accomplished in musical composition and who were already consciously engaged with a particular problem. Only someone who formally understood musical chords could actually *hear* 'the pure triad of E flat major' and only someone who had mastered the art of composition in his own culture could musically record it. The music from the dream trance has a noticeably nineteenth century sound. One surmises it would have sounded differently in any other century!

The examples I took from writing tell a similar story. Mary Shelley in her account tells her readers that before the trance-dream in which she saw Frankenstein and the monster, she had been discussing both ghost stories and recent scientific discoveries with her close friends who were also, as a kind of literary game, set on writing some new stories. The *genre* is there ('some volumes of ghost stories translated from the German into French fell into our hands ... "We will each write a ghost story", said Lord Bryon, and his proposition was acceded to.' [23]) The *theme* is there ('They talked of the experiments of Dr Darwin ... Perhaps a corpse would be reanimated; galvanism had given to them the idea of such things; perhaps the component parts of a creation might be manufactured ...'[24]) And a conducive *social context* existed ('I busied myself to think of a story – a story to rival those which had excited us to this task ....' 'Have you thought of a story?' I was asked each morning and each morning I was forced to reply with a mortifying negative.'[25])

In the case of R.L. Stevenson's *Dr Jekyll and Mr Hyde* the author assures us that he had 'long been trying to write a story on this subject' and that 'all the rest was made awake, and consciously'.[26] In this conscious-making of art (or science or theory) all that has been culturally inherited and assimilated, consciously and unconsciously, plays its part. But even more pertinent to my theme is the way in which past formulations can provide the essential elements for the creation of the new. Mary Shelley's story takes its form from existing ghost stories and half creates a new genre (science fiction) for others to emulate and further transform. R.L. Stevenson's *Dr Jekyll and Mr Hyde* belong to the nineteenth century tradition of the novella. Even Katherine Mansfield's story, in which the narrative is given in dream, is yet couched in the characteristic style of its author with all the intended and unintended echoes of her elected literary predecessors.

R.G. Collingwood claimed that the work of art (like the work of science or theory) *belongs not to the author but to the culture*. In *The Principles of Art* Collingwood eloquently presented his case for the necessity of plagiarism:

> ... we must get rid of the conception of artistic ownership ... if
> an artist may say nothing except what he has invented by his

own sole efforts, it stands to reason he will be poor in ideas. If he could take what he wants wherever he could find it, as Euripedes and Dante and Michelangelo and Shakespeare and Bach were free, his larder would always be full, and his cookery might be worth tasting.[27]

It may be no accident that the term 'self-expression' (first coined in 1892) came to birth six years after the first Berne Convention providing the international terms for literary copyright. Yet *plagiarism* (with due qualifications) may well be a better guide than *self-expression* in the arts for certainly it was an essential prerequisite of the practice of Greek dramatists, Renaissance painters and Elizabethan poets; indeed of all traditional art-making.

Our reflections on the horizontal axis of creativity, brief as they have been, lead us towards a recognition of the place of exemplars and models, to an appreciation of Winnicott's assertion that 'it is not possible to be original except on a basis of tradition',[28] and to a positive view of the place of imitation, creative theft, and productive plagiarism. A good tale can take a million tellings and not thereby be exhausted. Aesthetic Modernism and educational Progressivism, in denying tradition and the place of inherited symbols, over the last few decades have badly eroded the necessary conditions for high creative achievement.

The Implications of the Argument for the Classroom

I have argued that the mind is inherently creative, inherently disposed to culture and pattern making, and that this creativity can be understood as a kind of indivisible double engagement with the inner and the outer, with the psychosomatic and the cultural-historical. The two axes always act in some kind of conjunction, too subtle for definitive description. In the act of creation we thus see a complex interaction between a vertical and a horizontal axis; between the conscious and unconscious, between tradition and innovation. Generalizing from our observations on the vertical axis we might coin the aphorism: *No progression without regression!* Generalizing from the horizontal axis we might say: *No creation without tradition!* or *No transformation without the continuous internalization of conventions!* To begin to understand creativity we need to envisage a dialectical movement between these two axes in a dynamic model of the symbol-making mind. Perhaps the main value of such an analysis is that it may help us to recognize the nature of creativity and to provide the proper structural conditions for its development. I want to conclude by considering some of the implications of my argument for the teaching of the arts in our hugely uncreative schools.

In considering the development of creativity in the arts we must then keep constantly in mind two major axes and their moments of intersection. As teachers, we have to keep in touch with the biological roots of art-making, that conversion of impulse and feeling and mood into symbolic form, that obscure, interior movement that animates, connects and spontaneously creates inner figurative and narrative patterns. We have, in other words, to keep in touch with the rhythm of the body and the unconscious. *This is to follow the line of the vertical axis.*

At the same time, we have to draw on and draw in the inherited culture, all the artefacts that relate to the particular art discipline, all the techniques that have been laboriously evolved, and as much of the relevant discourse as can be understood and, perhaps, even more than can be immediately understood. (I am convinced that conceptually and culturally we have pitched the arts too low in our educational system.) This is to follow the rhythm of the horizontal axis, connecting the individual to the culture and the culture to the individual.

Our understanding of creativity calls for a complex, dialectical mode of teaching in which the teacher is constantly switching from one axis to another. In the tension created between them the creative act develops and takes its symbolic shape within the culture. The teacher of the arts has to acquire an agile intuitive sense as to which movement to make along which axis. Sometimes, for example, it is necessary not to interfere, to allow the crazy dream modality its freedom and inventiveness. A kind of anarchy! Allowing, permitting; and no judgments, no censorship. 'Let us learn to dream.'[29]

At other times, it is necessary for the teacher to actually teach, to positively introduce the nature of a form, its historical development and diverse usage, or to prescriptively draw attention to a particular technique or a critical concept. Here it is a matter of 'Let us learn to labour': to use materials, to test techniques, to raid the wealth of the past, to consciously make the work of art. In the first case then, emphasis is on the inner and the unconscious. In the second, on the cultural inheritance, the critical discourse, the set task. The final aim is to let these complementary polarities create the aesthetic field in the classroom within which our own biological creativity can flourish and develop. This is to advocate neither traditional prescriptive teaching nor child-centred progressive teaching. I would argue that such a method incorporates the productive sides of both models and forms a higher synthesis.

In this structural pattern, dialectical and complementary, deeply implicating the conscious and the unconscious, the body and the mind (the psychesoma), culture, community and history, lies the best paradigm for both the teaching of the arts and the general development of the innate and latent potentialities of our own complex natures. I believe that such a notion of creativity, with its promise of recreation and of renewal, is central to any animating definition of aesthetic education. It indicates a way beyond Modernism (with all its confining influences) and the way beyond government inspired Instrumentalism which so easily corrupts the essential meaning of educational activity.

Notes

1. WINNICOTT, D.W. (1971) *Playing and Reality*, Tavistock, p. 99.
2. Hugh Walpole quoted in BROOK, S. (Ed) (1983) *The Oxford Book of Dreams*, Oxford University Press, p. 85.
3. Locke, *An Essay Concerning Human Understanding*, abridged and edited by WILBURN, R. (1947), London, J.M. Dent, p.26.
4. S.T. Coleridge in a letter to Thomas Poole dated 16 October 1797 in POTTER, S. (Ed) (1962) *Coleridge Selected Poetry and Prose*, Nonesuch Press, p. 532.
5. GOMBRICH, E. (1979) *The Sense of Order: A Study in the Psychology of Decorative Art*, Phaidon, p. 14.
6. J. Z. Young quoted in BERGER J. (1962) *Art and Revolution*, Penguin, p. 112.
7. HARDY, B. (1975) *Tellers and Listeners*, Athlone Press, p. 3.
8. See KOESTLER, A. (1975) *The Act of Creation*, Picador, pp. 171–2.
9. *Ibid.*
10. LANGER, S. (1972) *Mind: An Essay on Human Feeling Volume 2*, John Hopkins Press, p. 286.
11. *Ibid*, p. 288.
12. *Ibid*, p. 289.
13. TIPPETT, M. (1974) *Moving Into Aquarius*, Paladin, p. 54.
    Michael Tippett elaborates as follows:

> that is, I *saw* a stage picture (as opposed to hearing a musical sound) of a wooded hilltop with a temple, where a warm and soft young man was being rebuffed by a cold and hard young woman (to my mind a very common present situation) to such a degree that the collective magical archetypes take charge – Jung's *anima* and *animus* – the girl, inflated by the latter, rises through the stage, flies to heaven, and the man, overwhelmed by the former,

descends through the stage floor to hell. But it was clear they would soon return. For I saw the girl later descending in a costume reminiscent of the goddess Athena (who was born without mother from Zeus's head) and the man ascending in one reminiscent of the god Dionysus (who, son of earth-born Semele, had a second birth from Zeus's thigh).

14. Account of the creation of the orchestral introduction to Wagner's *Rheingold* quoted by STORR (1983) 'Individuation and the creative process', *Journal of Analytical Psychology*, p. 337.
15. SHELLEY, M. (1968) Introduction to *Frankenstein*, Minister Classics, pp 12–13.
16. R.L. Stevenson quoted in BROOK, S. (Ed.) (1983) *op cit*, p. 138.
17. Katherine Mansfield quoted in *ibid*, p. 140.
18. Kekulé quoted in KOESTLER, A. (1975) *op cit*, p. 118.
19. Coleridge quoted in WHALLEY, G. (1974) 'Coleridge's poetic sensibility' in BEER, J. (Ed.) *Coleridge's Variety*, Macmillan, p. 15.
20. Quoted in review of *Coleridge: The Collected Works Vol I.* in *Times Literary Supplement*, 16 October 1987.
21. See Tate Gallery (1980) *Francis Bacon*, London, Tate Gallery.
22. In ECKERMANN's (n.d.) *Conversations with Goethe*, trs. by MOON, R.A. Morgan Laird & Co.
23. SHELLEY, M. (1968) *op cit*, pp. 8–9.
24. *Ibid*.
25. *Ibid*.
26. R.L. Stevenson quoted in BROOK, S. (Ed.) (1983) *op cit*.
27. COLLINGWOOD, R.G. (1958) *The Principles of Art*, Oxford University Press, p. 325.
28. WINNICOTT, D.W. (1971) *op cit*.
29. Kekulé quoted in KOESTLER, A. (1975) *op cit*.

Chapter 2
A Formal Aesthetic for the Teaching of the Arts

I laboured at a solid foundation on which permanently to ground my opinions in the component faculties of the human mind itself, and their comparative dignity and importance.

S.T. Coleridge

Any miscarriage of the symbolic process is an abrogation of our human freedom.

Susanne Langer

Beloved, at this moment let mind, knowing, breath, form, BE INCLUDED.

from Zen Flesh, Zen Bones

Preamble

Modernism and Progressivism, working in tandem, tended to deny what we called in the last chapter the horizontal axis of creativity; they tended to negate the need for a received culture (the richer the better) and the need for a prolonged apprenticeship in the inherited techniques of art-making. Now there is a movement at work in education to locate and release the suppressed elements of tradition and expressive technique in order to establish a comprehensive aesthetic for our schools. The aim is to restore the horizontal axis of creativity and bring it into dynamic relation with the vertical axis. In this chapter my aim is to define and defend this current shift in our understanding of the arts and their teaching. The shift entails a significant departure from an informal, essentially progressive and modernist approach, towards a more formal though structurally dynamic, aesthetics. As I will try to show, this formal aesthetics includes the progressive's emphasis on freedom and emotion but places it in a much larger and much more demanding pattern.

As the shift I am describing is registered most obviously in the influential *Gulbenkian Report: The Arts in Schools* (1982) I will begin my analysis with the philosophy of that document. I will then place the argument of the report in a tradition from which it largely derives. Finally, I will end by briefly considering some of the immediate implications of such a formal aesthetic for the teaching of the six great arts – music, literature, dance, drama, film and art – in our schools. I make no apology for the level of abstraction. Given the demand 'clarify or disappear', teachers of the arts have no choice but to embrace the challenge and set about the exacting task of intellectual clarification. Such an art of clarification can become the means not only of defence but also of affirmation; it can become, as I hope to show, the path to a much needed practical renewal and reorientation of the aesthetic disciplines in the classroom and studio. Even given the severe restraints of the National Curriculum, such a renewal is not out of the question. It is still possible for the enlightened school to give around 30 per cent of its time to the arts. This would entail the drawing together of English (see Chapters 3 and 4), Music, Design and Art (foundation subjects) and Dance and Drama (taken from the optional list of subjects). Indeed, from the point of view of this chapter, no school can be enlightened which fails to do so.

Art as Knowing: The Importance of the Gulbenkian Report

The concept of art as a form of knowing strongly informs the *Gulbenkian Report: The Arts in Schools*. It is frequently asserted there that art represents human rationality, is a mode of intelligence, is an act of enquiry or investigation, a form of thinking, a way of understanding. Such an epistemological conception of art would seem to be implicitly set against what can be roughly characterized as the progressive's conception of art, which tends to be child-centred rather than symbol-centred and committed to emotional development through self-expression rather than to the transpersonal representation of meaning through the language of a particular artistic medium. Even creativity, that all but magical word in the vocabulary of progressive education, is formally defined by the *Gulbenkian Report* as 'a form of intelligence' which can be 'developed and trained like any other mode of thinking'.[1]

Such a formulation, again, insists on the cognitive nature of creativity and strikes at that view which would see it as somehow ineffable, mysterious, wholly inexplicable. Elsewhere the *report* claims that creativity requires for its development 'a firm grounding in knowledge'.[2] The *Report* can thus be seen to both represent and further promote a considerable shift in educational thinking about the arts in this country; this shift involves a dramatic movement from informal child–centred naive 'expressive' conceptions of art towards a more formal aesthetic. I want now to explore the historical and philosophical background to this formal aesthetic before outlining some of its implications for the teaching of the arts.

The notion of art as a form of knowing is presented somewhat schematically in the *Gulbenkian Report* as the necessary outcome of a more general theory of knowledge which is radically pluralistic in nature and in opposition to the dominant conception of rationality in Western culture. What is needed, the *report* indicates, is the transformation of our concept of knowing so that it becomes inclusive of all the diverse ways in which we know and make a human world. The argument, by no means new, runs like this. In the Western world since the time of the Greek philosophers and particularly since the Renaissance, there has developed a powerful assumption that it is through the power of analytical reason, expressing itself in clear propositional forms, that we come to understand the nature of the world, that we come to valid knowledge. Abstract reason, working through a series of unambiguous propositions, linked to the principle of verification, (through which the propositions are tested for their truth or falsehood) has been given an all but exclusive power to define meaning and truth. In *An Essay Concerning Human Understanding* John Locke stated the central tenet as follows:

> ... certainty of knowledge is to perceive the agreement or disagreement of ideas as expressed in any proposition. This we usually call knowing as being certain of the truth of any proposition.[3]

Such a productively fertile but strangely constricted concept of knowledge and truth is recorded again and again in the philosophical tradition: from Bacon to Locke, from Locke to Mill, from Mill to the early Wittengstein and A.J. Ayer.

In a sense, what happened in Western civilization is that the Greek metaphysical logos became operationalized, with the result that theory had led more and more not to abstract contemplative understanding but

Plate 7   Castle Hill County Junior School, Basingstoke
We have not sufficiently analyzed the aesthetic significance of school buildings. These two modern schools, built within half a mile of each other, express radically different concepts of relationship, knowledge and meaning.

Plate 8   Fort Hill School and Community Centre, Basingstoke.

to the material organization and control of nature and society. Operational rationality is concerned, to repeat the famous and infamous words of Francis Bacon, with the effecting of all things possible and with the Empire of Man over Things. Thus, reason in Western Civilization has, in large measure, become contracted to an operational rationality based on the power of the proposition, backed by the method of empirical verification and fuelled by the appetite for accumulation and power. The micro-cosmic realization of this on the school is not difficult to discern. Consider, for example, the obsession with transactional language, with information, with quantitative measurement, with competitive achievement. Consider the absence of life-enhancing symbols in the school environment. Consider those bleak, numbered, rectangular classrooms where the lifeless desks and chairs are mechanically lined up to face the blackboard and the teacher's desk. Or, to come closer to our main theme, consider the isolated and undervalued position of the arts. Given the dominant notion of instrumental reason and given its further dilution in the confused institutions of mass education, such 'realities' seem inevitable, the daily surface manifestations of a theory of knowledge and (implicitly) value which underpin our complex technological and materialistic society.

The *Gulbenkian Report*, of course, does not deny the value of analytical reason or the verification principle or, in its appropriate place, an operational cast of mind. What, in its opening philosophical chapters, it seeks to challenge is the adequacy of the epistemology. Given a theory of knowledge confined to propositional forms, to logical and empirical methods, it is understandable that the arts in our schools came to be conceived in the manner of safety valves, mechanisms for the release of energy in order to return to the more fundamental work of rational and empirical understanding (however diluted). Strangely, the progressive's approach to art, by emphasising 'self-expression' and personal therapy, further buttressed such a view. Progressivism was the other half of Positivism – both were predicated on a radical dissociation between reason and feeling, logic and expression, public and private, objective and subjective. The *Gulbenkian Report* in contrast, is committed to reclaiming reason, to expanding its points of reference, to confer upon it a further range of movements, a wider variety of symbolic forms. The *report* celebrates 'the richness and variety' of rationality and rejects the prevailing exclusiveness of its current usage:

We reject the view that the only valid kinds of knowledge are

> those that are open to deductive reasoning and empirical tests ...
> The aesthetic, the religious and the moral realms are quite as
> powerful as those others in conveying knowledge. In our view
> public education has been too devoted to particular kinds of
> knowledge at the expense of others which are of equal impor-
> tance.[4]

Although the noun 'knowledge' here is in danger of suggesting a dead
corpus – rather, corpse – of 'received knowledge' rather than denoting
an act of knowing within a particular symbolic form, the demand for a
more comprehensive definition of reason remains clear. It is a demand,
as Louis Arnaud Reid has pointed out, that can be further supported by
a simple analysis of common linguistic usage for we use the verb 'to
know' to refer to knowing people (relational knowledge) as well as
works of art (aesthetic knowledge), to knowing what is morally right
action (ethical knowledge) as well as knowing the answer to a
mathematical problem (deductive knowledge) and knowing the outcome of an empirical experiment (scientific knowledge). Such a radical
pluralist expansion of epistemology, if widely understood and largely
endorsed, would have a dramatic bearing on the way we envisage the
school curriculum, not least on the place of the arts within it.

It is pertinent to note that the argument sketched in the *Gulbenkian
Report* has a striking affinity with that developed in Howard Gardner's
recent book *Frames of Mind*, subtitled *The Theory of Multiple Intelligences*.
Against the standard notion of a single kind of I.Q. (still obsessively
measured, if rather secretly, in our schools), Howard Gardner proposes
at least six kinds of active intelligence: linguistic, musical, logical-
mathematical, spatial, bodily-kinaesthetic and personal intelligence. He
argues that these 'frames of mind' are relatively autonomous, innate
proclivities of the mind which interact and develop with the symbolic
material in the culture. As with the *Gulbenkian Report*, the theory
demonstrates a dramatic movement from singular to plural forms of
reason:

> Only if we expand and reformulate our view of what counts as
> human intellect will we be able to devise more appropriate ways
> of assessing it and more effective ways of educating it.[5]

The notion of six forms of intelligence, however provisional,
however open to necessary qualification and, perhaps, addition and
reformulation, still compels us to examine the practice of our schools
with a kind of shock. It would seem that we develop in any significant

way only two of the six modes, the linguistic (and that only on the discursive side) and the logical-mathematical. The other forms of intelligence, musical, spatial, bodily-kinaesthetic and personal – remain at the most rudimentary level in most of our primary schools and in virtually all of our comprehensives. It is no accident that all those forms are intimately related to aesthetic education, to kinds of symbolism which are not propositional in nature. Perhaps, then, a real educational debate in this country, conducted by educationalists and teachers, and not politicians, should have been about multiple intelligences and the curriculum, about the various symbolic forms of the questing mind and their articulation and refinement in our schools? As it is, the present massive and barbaric retreat into 'basics' and the mechanical demand for standardized testing avoid all the primary educational questions. The theory of multiple intelligences, or what in this paper we will call symbolic forms, may well be, as Howard Gardner claims, an idea whose time has come, but the actual context for its application could hardly be more uninvitingly bleak. Yet Gardner's *Frames of Mind* and the *Gulbenkian Report* are not isolated publications. They belong, in large part, to a Kantian and post-Kantian tradition of thinking which art-teachers, in the present educational crisis, need to be aware of.

The Intellectual Tradition

It was Kant who in his 1786 Preface to the second edition of the *Critique of Pure Reason* wrote 'experience itself is a mode of cognition which requires understanding'.[6] Experience, Kant claimed, is not simply given, it is made through the active powers of the mind, and in *The Critique* he sought to define those innate *a priori* categories through which we structure what we know. The two purposes of his formidably difficult book, to deduce 'in the analytic' the number of the categories and in 'the dialect' to show their unjustified employment in traditional metaphysics, do not concern us here. What is important to notice is the primacy given to the mind in constructing experience and the emerging theory of forms or 'frames' of knowing. Kant, in the preface to the second edition, offered a brief historical reconstruction of logic, mathematics, natural science and metaphysics. He suggested also that if we could grasp the inherent structures of the mind we should be able to arrive at a complete enumeration of the mind's possible modes for proposing problems to itself. In the *Critique* his concern is to ground Newtonian science in the permanent conditions of the mind in order 'to clear and level a fit foundation for the scientific edifice'[7] but *the principle* for a much greater structural elaboration of symbolic categories is there. For if there are innate categories mediating our experience, could there not also be (as Jung was later to insist) *a priori* images, *a priori* narratives, *a priori* genres? Could not the Kantian method be extended to include all forms of culture, including a formal analysis of all the arts? It was Ernst Cassirer who took the principle of Kant's transcendental analytic, the deduction of the antecedent categories, and brought it to an understanding of language, myth, religion, the arts, as well as mathematics and science, to create a comprehensive semiotics, a philosophy of symbolic forms. This philosophy was particularly in tune with Romanticism for that movement was also preoccupied with the autonomy of art and the creative agency of the mind. Art was no longer seen as mimetic in the sense of representing faithfully a fixed outer order but more as an energy of imagination which unfolded, according to its poetic grammar, the inherent laws of its gestation and expression. The insights of the structuralists, inspired by Saussure, also belong to this same post-Kantian current, for Saussure's perceptions that it is the systematic relationship *between words* rather than their referentiality which makes communication possible, assert once more the primacy of the symbol over the object or, as it came to be named, of the signifier over the signified. All the symbols of culture and art could now be studied not only in terms of historical process and authorial intentionality but also in terms of the function of the mind which created them and in terms of their own informing rules and possibilities. This is what Roland Barthes called the structuralist activity. I want now to examine the general framework for this aesthetic proposed by Susanne Langer.

Susanne Langer developed further the work of Ernst Cassirer. In *Feeling and Form*, dedicated to her philosophical mentor, she wrote her own critique, this time not of pure reason and its conceptual apparatus but of mind as it manifested itself in the symbolism of the arts. It is not the place to review this seminal work, but in order to take further the notion of art as a form of knowing it is necessary to briefly delineate Langer's important distinctions between signal and symbol as well as between discursive symbolism and non-discursive symbolism. This second distinction is of crucial significance in understanding the way in which the arts transcend pure subjectivity and self-expression. Once the idea of non-discursive meaning has been grasped we are in a position to turn to the teaching of the arts with a new angle of perception and an enriched sense of formal possibilities. The following diagram may help by indicating the basic terms and suggesting schematically the drift of the argument:

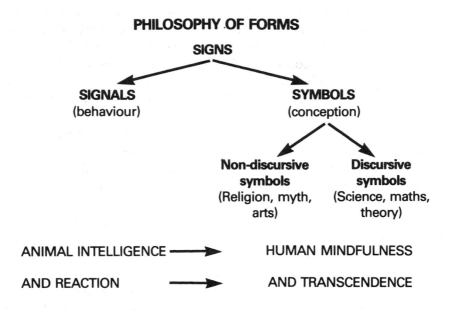

PHILOSOPHY OF FORMS

According to Susanne Langer we share with animals our ability to make signals, while our ability to make symbols remains distinctly human, the hallmark of *homo sapiens.*

It is the function of the signal simultaneously to refer to something and to release in the person or animal a predictable behavioural reaction. The bell rings to announce food; the dog salivates and moves to its eating bowl. The traffic lights in front of me turn to amber and red; I slow down and bring the car to a stop. The reactions are automatic, predictable, uniform. There is a fixed mechanical relationship, however arbitrary the sign, between the signal and the response. As soon as the behaviour has been released, the signal is forgotten: it has served its biological or social purpose. Signals are adaptive; through their unambiguous reference they stimulate functionally valuable reactions. tionally valuable reactions.

In contrast, symbols, which Langer characterizes as any devices which make abstraction possible, *conceive* a world and engender not so much reactions as reflection. Signals are mindless, we might say, whereas symbols are mindful. Human kind employs signs not only to signal needed action but also to represent, *re-present* and conceive.

Thus the symbol, unlike the signal, records and makes possible a kind of transcendence over the phenomenal world. The power to create symbols creates a psychic space within the natural space, a psychic time within natural time, where through the play of mind upon its own symbolic constructs, the possibility of meaning is established. For Langer, as for Cassirer, the symbolic transformation of experience is the primary and virtually continuous activity of the human mind. We are symbol-making, symbol-mongering animals. And, as Kant indicated, we mediate our human world all but unconsciously through their spontaneous operation.

Wherever there is a symbol, a certain conception is in formation – but these conceptions are not necessarily of the same kind. Langer, as we have seen, divides symbols into two large categories, the discursive and the non-discursive. The discursive symbols are analytical in nature and sequential in movement. They work through precision of reference and gravitate towards the abstract and general. In fact, discursive symbolism is the characteristic and necessary symbolism of the operational mind, which we described earlier as the dominant mode of thinking in our technological society. It is the symbolism of science and the humanities, of all organized research and rational enquiry. It is a mark of discursive symbolism that it can be translated into other signs without loss of meaning:

$$2 + 2 = 4$$

two and two equals four

$$II + II = IV$$

In these different styles, or indeed translated into any number of different languages, the essential discursive meaning still remains constant. In contrast, in non discursive symbols – the symbols of dream, myth, religion, art – the meaning is inextricably embedded in the specific symbolic formulation and cannot be extracted without diminution. The meaning, say, of Beethoven's *Grosse Fuge* or Chagall's *Lovers in the Lilac* or Elizabeth Frink's *Harbinger Bird III 1961* cannot exist in any other way. There are no other equivalent systems into which their meanings can be transposed. Whatever value or universality they possess they hold within the uniqueness of their structural forms. Their meanings are embodied in the symbols and it is only in response to those actual symbols that they can be truly understood. Thus, for Langer, non-discursive symbols bear conception (particularly the conception of feelings and sentience) and engender reflection but in a radically different manner from that, say, of science or mathematics. The symbols of art serve to bring sentience, emotion, feeling, aspiration to consciousness by artistically embodying them in such a way that they are understood in any more-or-less adequate aesthetic response to them. Langer writes:

> The recognition of presentational (non-discursive) symbolism as a normal and prevalent vehicle of meaning widens our conception of rationality far beyond the traditional boundaries yet never breaks faith with logic in the strictest sense. Wherever a symbol operates, there is a meaning; and, conversely, different classes of experience – say, reason, intuition, appreciation – correspond to different types of symbolic mediation. No symbol is exempt from the office of logical formulation, of *conceptualizing* what it conveys; however simple its import, or however great, this import is a *meaning*, and therefore an element for understanding.[8]

Her argument eloquently phrased, returns us to the *Gulbenkian Report* and its urgent plea for a more adequate epistemology. It becomes transparently clear that if the post-Kantian position of (among many others) Ernst Cassirer and Susanne Langer is, in its general import, convincing then what our educational system has failed to attend to is the power of non-discursive symbolism in creating and formulating meaning and value. There is no symbolic balance or equity in the current curriculum. All the non-linguistic forms of knowing are neglected, and even the linguistic forms are mostly confined to the linear and the discursive. Here then is the challenge to the general curriculum. But there is a second challenge, and that is the challenge to the arts themselves; for it is this philosophy of symbolism which has given birth to that formal aesthetic which I mentioned at the outset of this chapter. I want now to reflect on some of the practical implications for the teaching of the arts. In part, our task as arts teachers is to lift the structuralist activity into the expressive, aesthetic realm in the classroom and studio. But this is to anticipate ...

The Transformation of Aesthetic Practices in our Schools

The interest in symbolism urges us as arts teachers to consider more fully the formal possibilities of each expressive medium. It urges us to become more aware, more systematically conscious of the grammar of art, of techniques of conventions, of traditions. It engenders a sensitivity to genre and to what I will call 'symbolic field', namely that complex magnetic system of reference and allusion, of stylistic attraction and repulsion, within which any individual work of art is, both consciously and unconsciously, constituted. For art, as was argued in the last chapter, not only emerges from the raw emotions and impulses of the art-maker, it also emerges under many diverse influences, from other art. God may create *ex nihilo*, but not the art-maker. Both for the maker and the receiver, art presupposes other works of art; it assumes tacit understandings, implicit conventions, shared reference points within the symbolic field. Iconoclasm, paradoxically, depends absolutely for its meaning on an understanding of the tradition it appears to destroy; its power depends on what it rejects. Iconoclasm, limited as it often is, does not destroy the field but extends it and, more fundamentally, re-establishes it. This complex system of inner pointing and counter-pointing is most dramatically at work in early Modernism: the work of Joyce, Pound, Eliot, Yeats depend upon its recognition. What can *The Waste Land* mean to those who do not recognize at least some of the quotations and references which make up the direct textual montage of the poem? In a not dissimilar manner painters like Picasso and Bacon have, at times, quoted and reframed the paintings of the past. And, indeed, informing nearly the whole of Western art, as a configuring energy are the parables and metaphors of the Bible and the images and narratives of Greek mythology. To develop in our pupils an appreciation of the aesthetic field of each art discipline is not only to increase their individual grasp of many specific works of art, it is also to extend the expressive possibilities of their own art-making. It would seem that we have often failed to create any such knowledge in our pupils. In English teaching, there has been too much preoccupation with social realist texts and the discussion of their 'message', too little concern with the symbolic nature of literature, its traditions, conventions and possibilities. Even the emphasis on contemporary texts has narrowed the range of reference and indicated only a small number of ways in which through language worlds of meaning can be created. In many other expressive disciplines – notably in dance and, to a lesser extent, drama – the obsession with 'self expression' (rather than 'art-expression') has also tended to exclude a knowledge of technique and convention which alone can develop and refine the expressive potential of the art-maker. Imitation is not the enemy of spontaneity, knowledge is not the enemy of creativity; rather they are the means to develop both appreciation and

Plate 9   Arnult Rainer Wine Crucifix 1957|78
Informing so much art, as a configuring energy, are the metaphors of the Bible. In this modern painting one senses both the biological sources of art-making in instinctive gestures and also the deep cultural sources of Christianity.

production. Creative plagiarism is at least one half of the art-making process. The immersion of our pupils in the symbolic field of the expressive medium we teach must be one of our primary aims. Our task is to imaginatively introduce the various grammars of non-discursive symbolism.

How can this be done? If we accept the notion of non-discursive symbolism it follows that to develop an adequate response to the meaning of art we must use teaching methods that keep the response of our pupils in the aesthetic mode, deepening it and refining it. The logic of our tactics must be in intimate relationship to the kind of symbolism we are committed to. The grammar of the arts, therefore, cannot be introduced through a series of prescribed schematic exercises divorced from the animating energies of feelings, sense perception and imagination. They must be introduced as a necessary part of *expressive activity seeking formal articulation*. In the study of literature, for example, teachers too frequently encourage discursive reactions about content so that the pupil is directed almost from the outset to think outside rather than inside the very medium she is studying. Once again we detect here the inordinate power of the discursive to confer educational respectability. If the teacher says, 'Write an essay about it!' it is considered serious; if, however, the teacher struggles to keep the activity in the aesthetic mode ('read the poem on tape', 'imitate the form', 'close the poem in an alternative way') then it is invariably felt that something 'soft' and 'easy' is being called for. It is, of course, significant that the art of oral rendering (including the art of adapting and performing literary work) is neglected in our schools, and hardly exists at all in the study of literature at our universities. The knowledge of the symbolic field is best imparted through direct aesthetic engagement with many different genres, through an imaginative involvement with their meanings, as well as a practical pre-occupation with both their metaphors and structures seen as possible material for further symbolic re-creation in terms of personal and contemporary experience. The art-teacher's task is to promote that reciprocal play between the repertoire of artistic conventions inherited through the culture and that innate proclivity in the individual and group for symbolic expression. The formal aesthetics we have proposed, then, would have the arts taught as *aesthetic activity* where the conventions of art and the meanings of art are grasped through the medium of art and through sustained practical experience of art-making. At times, close conceptual analysis, historical knowledge, ideological knowledge, biographical knowledge, will be necessary for understanding, at times, careful interpretive essays may be called for; but, essentially, aesthetic disciplines should be rooted in the sensuous, analogical, poetic non-discursive mode of knowing. For there lies their distinctive characteristic. There also, as many arts-teachers can testify, lies their transformative educational power.

The principle of employing non-discursive forms for the teaching of non-discursive symbols (a principle far from alien to the current practice of teaching dance, drama and the visual arts, but rather removed from the teaching of English, music and film) generates a further notion, that of the teacher as co-artist. The practice of good art college teaching, where the teacher paints alongside the students, establishes a ready model for what I have in mind. According to this model, the teacher of an arts discipline becomes, in some measure, a practitioner: the music teacher composes, the teacher of literature writes and edits, the teacher of dance dances, and all should be ready, at times, to act as creative exemplars. But there is a further related, more subtle aspect to the notion of co-artist; it is the function of the arts-teacher not only to initiate aesthetic activity but also to enter it directly as creative agent, to develop it and deepen it. This is a most problematic area. In the past, in some of the arts, teachers have been peculiarly reluctant to enter the creative act of the pupil. They have been ready to start the artistic process and then have uneasily stood back and waited, power-less observers of the mystery of creativity, or, more often, the anxious observers of lost and ship-wrecked souls clinging to whatever obscure flotsam they can find. As co-artist, one of the responsibilities of the arts-teacher is to enter the creative process of the class and, where necessary, alter it structurally in terms of its latent aesthetic possibilities. Dorothy Heathcote evolved, through her own practice of drama teaching, a most effective method for securing creative intervention into the drama process. For Heathcote, the drama teacher must be both organizer and also, at critical moments, co-dramatist. The drama teacher moves from one role to the other in terms of what the art-making requires. As organizer the teacher can stand back and inspect with the sharp eye of an outsider; as co-dramatist, she can adopt a dramatic part (say, that of a messenger) and enter the symbolic action of the pupils' drama. By entering the action 'in role' she has the power to free the creative process from sudden blocks, or the inertia of accruing clichés and stereotypes. As soon as the pupils' art-making has been realized, she can unobtrusively switch back into the role of the teacher. The dual role thus employed allows for the creative entry of the teacher into the art process without any break in the symbolic medium. It is a most fertile conception and could, no doubt, be extended, with various modifications, across all the aesthetic disciplines. Such a prin-ciple of creative intervention in the artistic medium requires immense integrity and a sensitive feeling for aesthetic form. Used with sen-sitivity, Heathcote's technique becomes an instrument for the develop-ment of artistic work much needed after a long period of *laisser-faire* and the often uncritical acceptance of all creative work (however poor) as sacerdotal manifestations of the inviolable self.

Explicit throughout this chapter has been the conception that the arts adhere; that, for all their tangible differences, they belong funda-mentally to the same symbolic community. In the context of teaching, the arts share the twin concerns for the appreciation of art and the production of art; they assume the same kind of creative process, moving from the exploratory stage of drafting through to the realiza-tion of symbolic form and the presentation of that form to an actual audience; they are also all committed, as we have argued, to non-propositional forms of symbolism. Nevertheless, the arts in our schools have remained sharply segregated and woefully ignorant of each other. This in turn has further weakened them and made them organizationally ineffectual whenever there have been questions of cuts and priorities. It has also blocked many possibilities of active collaboration in teaching. In English, for example, kinetic poetry runs into visual design, the ballad runs into music, the study of Shakespeare runs into theatre, drama and dance – but because of the inheritance of a provincial and guarded isolation, these possibilities are rarely developed into collaborative enquiry. More generally, the emerging formal aesthetic calls for an end to the *ad hoc* jumble of largely ill-conceived art specialism in the curriculum and the beginning of an arts community committed to a sustained aesthetic education for all our pupils through all the major art forms. We need to establish a practice which does justice to the partial autonomy of each expressive discipline while recognizing their place in the arts community as a whole, sharing that common pursuit to give expressive form to life and, in so doing, to contemplate its possibilities and purposes. This calls for a major reconstruction of the curriculum; it also suggests that the symbols produced in the classroom-studio should not be confined there, but taken out into the environment of the school and beyond that into the community, which the school exists to serve both artistically and intellectually.

Conclusion

Our formal aesthetic, then, returns us to life. 'Aesthetic' in our context, means *artistic activity*; and 'formal' refers to those structural forms which are the *poetic grammar of the life of feeling and imagination.* In the arts we could say, in Kantian style, that feeling without form cannot be comprehended, and that form without feeling has in it nothing worth comprehending. Susanne Langer claimed:

> Art is a public possession, because the formulation of felt-life is the heart of any culture and moulds the objective world for the people. It is their school of feeling and their defence against outer and inner chaos. [9]

Our argument for a formal aesthetic in the curriculum is, finally, an argument to establish the place of and a place for feeling; schools of feeling, indeed.

Notes

1. BRINSON, P. (Ed) (1982) *The Arts in Schools*, Calouste Gulbenkian Foundation, p. 29.
2. *Ibid.*
3. LOCKE, J. (1947) *An Essay Concerning Human Understanding*, J.M. Dent and Sons, p. 280.
4. BRINSON, P. (Ed) (1982) *op cit.* p. 24.
5. GARDNER, H. (1983) *Frames of Mind: The Theory of Multiple Intelligences*, Basic Books, p. 4.
6. KANT, I. *Critique of Pure Reason*, Dent and Sons, Preface to the 1787 Second Edition, p. 12.
7. *Ibid.* Preface to 1781 First Edition, p. 7.
8. LANGER, S. (1980) *Philosophy in a New Key: A Study in the Symbolism of Reason, Rite and Art*, Harvard University Press, p. 97.
9. LANGER, S. (1953) *Feeling and Form: A Theory of Art*, Routledge and Kegan Paul, p. 409.

Chapter 3
English as an Arts Discipline:
A Defence of English as an Aesthetic Discipline with special reference to the HMI document English 5-16

Preamble

Any comprehensive aesthetic programme for our schools must include English. Yet English has remained on the very edge of the arts debate, reluctant to become involved, reluctant to be, in any way, implicated. The very word 'aesthetic' is conspicuous by its absence in the discourse of English teachers. In this and the following chapter I, therefore, put the case for conceiving English as an aesthetic discipline, a literary-expressive discipline centred on perceptual and imaginative response.

Introduction

The recent HMI document *English from 5 to 16*, as a first step towards securing a national policy, offered a general framework for English teaching. In the penultimate paragraph of the document the following challenge was made.

> It is hoped, however, that it will at least provide a framework for general agreement about the aims, objectives and general principles of English teaching – or an incitement to others to provide a better framework. For present practice in the teaching of English in our schools varies greatly, and such agreement is urgently needed.[1]

In this chapter I wish to suggest an alternative framework to the one put forward by HMI, a framework which puts much greater emphasis on literature and expression, on imagination and feeling, on experiential process and personal development and does so in the context of a comprehensive aesthetic education. It is highly significant that in spite of a number of recent movements to draw English and the arts closer together, the HMI document does not employ the word 'aesthetic' once (the key word is 'competence'), nor does it refer once to the national arts debate inaugurated by the Gulbenkian Report *The Arts in Schools* (1982). Indeed, the HMI paper seems to float free of all the actual controversies in English – no mention of structuralism or post-structuralism, no mention of deconstruction or semiotics – as if there could be some easily achieved collective agreement without reference to these specific disputes which, at once, energize and splinter the English teaching community. It is a strangely ahistorical document. The anodyne listing of pseudo-empirical objectives such as (for the 11-year-old pupil) the ability to:

> Converse confidently and pleasantly in social situations.[2]
> Participate courteously and constructively in discussion.[3]
> Make confident and effective use of the telephone.[4]

can be no substitute for real argument. If there is controversy and confusion in English teaching (as there is), and if a national policy is needed, then these confusions have to be delineated and the controversies encountered and evaluated.

Of course, a report as general as *English from 5 to 16* inevitably puts forward notions and practices with which one has to generally agree. Thus the division of English into the four modes of writing, listening, speaking and reading (developed from *The Bullock Report*) has a certain value, as does the strong support for impression evaluation rather than the mechanical marking of pupils' work. And when the report states that 'good teaching of English, at any level, is far more than the inculcation of skills: it is an education of the intellect and sensibility' one wants to applaud, and yet the informing tone and the unambiguous direction of the report as a whole negates any such magnificent educational claim. The document leaves one with the enervating sense that English has no distinctive educational centre; leaves one with the notion that English teaching is a mere matter of taking on endless and disparate responsibilities, many of them instrumental in character. So many linguistic 'tasks' are expected that the appreciation and creation of literature becomes an all but minimal element in an infinitely larger linguistic equation. The claim for the education of intellect and sensibility sounds like specious rhetoric, a euphoric phrase plucked from a prior tradition of English teaching which, ironically, is only poorly represented in the report. One envisages the English teacher of tomorrow nervously clutching a dozen check-lists, not holding a contemporary novel or a batch of creative work from 3L. There is an amusing misprint on page four of the report where it is urged that teachers must equip their pupils with '*the rage* of competence in language'. Indeed there is a rage for 'competence' in the document (the word is used nine times in the first four pages) and a rage for tabulated objectives – and in this rage for externality it is difficult to see where the slow and often elusive development of sensibility and intellect belongs, or, even, how it could possibly take place.

To move towards a formulation of an alternative conception of English we need, first, a description and critique of recent theory and practice. To do this I will elaborate further the analysis I made in *English Within the Arts* (1982). I will, briefly, document the major trends in English teaching over the last two decades and, examining them, begin to draw out the premises of an arts approach to English studies. My case will depend upon a full recognition of the implications of a language across the curriculum policy. It will also depend upon an understanding of an emerging concern for a unified aesthetic education, expressed most recently in *The Arts in Schools* report and embodied dramatically in the recent foundation of the *National Association for Education in the Arts*. Both these seminal educational developments go unmentioned in the HMI report. Yet it is difficult to understand how there could ever be a convincing national policy for English teaching which had not taken cognizance of these educational challenges and considered their many ramifications for the whole curriculum.

My main argument will refer most often to secondary education and the responsibilities of the English Department. Nevertheless, the implications for primary schools should be clear. We are in danger of losing any serious commitment to those qualities of language which are personal, analogical, imagistic, aesthetic, which in terms of symbolic typology belong to myth and literature and, beyond that, to the expressive disciplines of art, drama, dance and music, all of which are shockingly underrepresented (or, even, not represented) in our educational system. To argue for English as an arts discipline is to argue for an aesthetic education. It is not, however, to argue against all the objectives listed by HMI; it is, as shall become clear, to see the responsibility for many of those objectives lying across the whole curriculum and with the teaching profession as a whole; it is also to argue the need for a balance between the different forms of symbolic enquiry so that the sensuous and imaginative forms of symbolism are not, as they are now, elbowed to one side by the discursive and the instrumental.

I will begin the analysis with a brief account and interpretation of recent trends in English teaching. In this way the HMI report can be placed in its historical context, as can the alternative conception of an arts approach to English.

English in the Sociolinguistic School

It is uncontentious to claim that the major preoccupation of English teaching during the late 1960s and 1970s was with language and learning. Informed by concepts deriving from linguistics and sociology, many English teachers concerned themselves with the intersections between language and social class, language and politics, language and the curriculum. References to different kinds of language (Was it poetic? Was it transactional? Was it expressive?) and to different kinds of coding (Was it in the so-called restricted code of the working class? Or the elaborate code of the middle-class?) were ubiquitous and began to predetermine the issues which characterized the serious discussion of English. The titles of some of the most widely disseminated books – *Language, the Learner and the School* (Barnes, 1969), *Language and Learning* (Britton, 1970), *The Language of Primary School Children* (Rosen and Rosen, 1973) revealed the breadth of interest. The concerns were linguistic and educational. Some of the most influential formulations were those relating to 'oracy' and 'language across the curriculum'. It is true that, in a sense, oracy had always been part of the classical conception of rhetoric and that a principle not dissimilar from language across the curriculum had been enunciated in George Sampson's *English for the English* (1921), where it was maintained that all teachers were, inevitably, teachers of the mother-tongue, teachers of English. However, these concepts were given a further urgency, a further reference and a new orientation. Oracy was no longer related to oratory or style in speaking but to an understanding of the various registers of language in integrating experience. English teachers listened more carefully to the actual languages their pupils used, in the corridor, in the playground, in the community, in large and small group discussions in the classroom. The concept of a single language for education was breaking down to a complex recognition of a mutliplicity of languages, all of which needed to be used and studied. Dialect for example, was, no longer seen as an inferior or bastardized form of a standard language but as an authentic pattern of expression and communication to be kept alive rather than exterminated by the red biro marks and the general disdain of the teaching profession; dialect was an essential manifestation of the innate heterogeneity of language in relationship to locality and community. At a more general level, the linguistic theory developed an increasing awareness of the intimate relationship between language and learning.

Some of the practical implications of such language awareness were put forward in *The Bullock Report* (1975):

> For language to play its full role as a means of learning, the teacher must create in the classroom an environment which encourages a wide range of language uses. The effectiveness of this context for the purpose can be judged by the answers to a number of questions. For example, how often does a child share his personal interests and learning discoveries with others in the class? How far is the teacher able to enter such conversations without robbing the children of verbal initiative? Are the children accustomed to read to one another what they have written, and just as readily listen? Are they accustomed to solving cooperatively in talk the practical problems that arise when they work together? How much opportunity is there for the kind of talk by which children make sense in their own terms of the information offered by teacher or by book? What varieties of writing – story, personal record, comment, report, speculation etc. – are produced in the course of a day?[5]

The many prescriptive grammar books, based on a static Latinate model of the English language, were seen to lack fitting application. The new emphasis was pragmatic rather than theoretical; the preoccupation was with the actual uses of language, the diverse ways in which it worked, particularly in its spoken forms. What was challenged was the inert notion of learning as the transmission of knowledge in text-book language from the teacher to the pupil. Learning was a grasping act of the mind, not a stamping of set formulae on the blank sheet of the brain. It can, perhaps, be seen how the HMI report *English from 5 to 16* has taken some of the central concerns of the sociolinguistic revolution – a concern for all kinds of language, a concern, in particular, for speech – but shorn them of their radical intent.

To a considerable extent the sociolinguistic writers erased the earlier traditions of English teaching, both the progressive tradition, perhaps best formulated by Marjorie Hourd in her *The Education of the Poetic Spirit* (1949), and the Cambridge School of English inspired by the works of F.R. Leavis and his teaching at Downing College. Intellectual movements in their own quiet manner can be bloody matters and often what has been destroyed can only be located by listing the omissions in seemingly harmless bibliographies. The progressive school had focused on the child as creative maker and the Cambridge School on the close examination of literary works; and it was precisely these literary and aesthetic elements which paradoxically the 'broad' concern with language was in danger of eclipsing. It was significant that of the 559 pages of the *Bullock Report* only nineteen pages were given to literature and no more than three paragraphs to poetry. The recent HMI report with its general language approach and its only occasional and then, rather bland references to literature and imaginative writing can be understood as the further development of a powerful trend to make literary experience a minor part of English studies.

As a specific discipline in the secondary curriculum, English began to lack unity. Eclectic anthologies made up of a mixture of photographs, excerpts, contemporary poems, without questions, without deep structure, without guidance, poured out from the publishers during the late 1960s and early 1970s. They were attractive visually but were often structurally amorphous. The dominant approach during this time was thematic and loosely ideological. Classroom work was integrated through a series of themes, generally social and political in nature; for stimuli it depended upon extracts culled from literature (often of a social realist kind), excerpts from newspapers and magazines. These extracts were the starting points from which one moved outwards into 'the issues'. Themes would include old age, crime, the family, war, social class, the neighbourhood. Whole anthologies were published around set themes; *Work and Leisure* (1968), *Loneliness and Parting* (1968), *Life in the City* (1969), *Love and Marriage* (1970). The word on the lips of teachers was 'relevance'. The word was not deeply excavated. It was automatically assumed that relevant meant *socially relevant* – something relevant was happening when one was grappling with direct social issues. The tasks set by the teacher would range from talking to small groups, to various kinds of research, to some personal writing, to discursive writing, to formal and informal comprehension (especially in the fourth and fifth years). The new informality encouraged a greater sense of pupil participation and, perhaps, also there was a greater sense of engagement because the pupils could bring quickly into the arena their own immediate social experience. Following the inevitable direc-

Plate 10 from the text-book Reflections. *In the 1960s and 1970s English often became integrated through themes which were social and ideological in nature.*

Plate 11 from Reflections. *In many influential text-books literature was seen as a transparent window onto a social universe.*

tion of such a current, a number of English departments, at least in the lower half of the secondary school, decided to merge with general *humanities* courses.

It is essential to note that at the same time as this shift was taking place, a certain disillusionment with what had been inadequately called 'creative writing' had become widespread. It was vaguely felt that 'self-expression' too easily deteriorated into 'self-effusion' and that the teacher had no practical way of engaging with such personal acts. *The Bullock Report* quoted the following extract from a teacher's document:

> Many teachers see 'creative writing' as the high point of literacy. We need to rethink this: over-emphasis on it has distorted a whole view of language, it usually means, in actuality, colourful or fanciful language not 'ordinary', using 'vivid imagery'. It is often false, artificially stimulated and pumped up by the teacher or written to an unconscious model which he has given to the children. It is very often divorced from real feeling.[6]

Without a widespread understanding of an arts approach in English the project was, perhaps, doomed to fail. Without reference to technique, without care for revision based on an awareness of the various stages of the creative process, without a sense of performance or an attentive audience, the direct art-making element in English, fostered by the earlier work of Marjorie Hourd and David Holbrook, tended to wither. Thus, around this time, a broadly thematic humanities style of approach or a further notion that English should be recast as linguistics, seemed both exciting and inevitable alternatives.

The preoccupation with language and learning, the concentration on social issues, the method of integrating work through a thematic approach, all this, coupled with the virtual denial of earlier traditions in English teaching, meant that certain crucial questions went unasked. What is a fitting approach to literature as literature? What are the connections between English and the other arts? What is the nature of the creative process in the arts? What is aesthetic education? These were questions of a seminal nature which were all but excluded by the linguistic and sociological preoccupations. Significantly, they remained unasked in the HMI report on English. The HMI's lack of conviction for the literary and aesthetic is revealed by their strange defensive habit of endlessly coupling the functional and the imaginative as, for example, in the following formulations:

> Such liberties (of young writers) with language need to be

accompanied by clear awareness of how and why accepted usage is being rejected and of what is needed in more utilitarian communications.[7]

The language resources used in a poem differ from and complement those used in a set of instructions for carrying out a process.[8]

Writing a business letter requires greater conciseness than writing a story.[9]

The anxiety is palpable. Yet there *has been* a significant move in English studies towards the literary and aesthetic; this movement has taken place erratically, around the edges of the sociolinguistic centre. Why, one wonders, have the authors of the HMI document failed to notice it, failed to refer to it? To complete this historical survey it is necessary to present a brief sketch of this arts movement within English.

The Aesthetic Movement Within English

For complex historical reasons the arts in education have always been divided; they have entered the curriculum at different times under the power of diverse conceptions and diverse pedagogies, under diverse political, material and organizational pressures and constraints. English, while constitutionally seen as one of the humanities, often included in its practice drama. (It is interesting to note that this connection survives in the HMI report: 'If in the secondary school there is a separate drama department, its work should be closely related to that of English; if not, drama work should be part of the English programme'.) It did not, however, forge working relationships with the visual arts, with film (where it existed) with music or (where it existed) dance. The Schools Council Project *Arts and the Adolescent*, set up in 1968, was pioneering in that, among other things, it sought to discover 'some formula for bringing work in the different art subjects into closer relationship both with each other and with the curriculum as a whole', and furthermore conceived the discipline of English as one of those art subjects.

The problematic position of the English teacher became quickly visible in the work of the project. In the report *Schools Council Working Paper 54* Malcolm Ross described his position as follows:

Thus, on reflection, the lot of the English teacher may not be as enviable as the prestige of his position would suggest. His can be a cruel dilemma: usually intensely interested in literature himself and firmly committed, in spirit at least, to the notion that an individual's language should reflect and extend his personality, he frequently has to lower his sights and 'make do' with his 'O' level improbables and the writing of formal letters with the ROSLA group. Shades of the prison house will darken the journals and poems and short stories of his young creative writers by the time they come to the end of their third year in secondary school. And he will be in no position to say why this should not be so.[10]

In the related volume *The Intelligence of Feeling* (1974) Witkin elaborated further on the possible reasons for the alienation of the English teacher from his creative function. By the very nature of his medium, Witkin argued, the English teacher became pulled into the dominant factual and impersonal discourse of the school and tended to falsely objectify the feelings of his pupils by simply converting them into material for discursive examination; the pupils' subjectivity was thus touched upon only to be converted into a series of propositions – opinions, values, issues, judgments – for general discussion. Witkin wrote:

> Within the context of the school curriculum verbal behaviour is very much the servant of objectivity. The curriculum is very largely devoted to the development of the object-centred perspective in the furtherance of rational action in the world. Subject-centred speech is often experienced as alarming because it makes claims upon the world that are independent of logical principles and rational action. These claims are often perceived as anarchical in origin to the extent that the intelligence of feeling is not comprehended by the teacher's praxis . . .

> Thus in discussing characters, passions or authors in English literature, pupils are encouraged to express their own subjective views in logical discourse about them. Passion is not to be met with passion in expression but with thoughts about passion . . .

> This contradiction only arises however to the extent that the creative process and the act of self-expression are not comprehended by the teacher's praxis and remain external to it. When this is no longer the case then the teacher's praxis will embrace the self-expression of the pupil in ways that will lead to the full use of verbal media in creative reading and creative

writing, and the use of English studies as the careful structuring of value judgments will decline.[11]

Rather than rush into the objective discursive mode, Witkin and Ross would have English teachers work within the unfolding feelings of their pupils, work so that the responses would not be turned into set positions for safe discussion but slowly elaborated through a personal struggle with language into expressive symbolic forms (*this* story, *this* poem, *these* metaphors being shaped messily as the pen moves across the page) or into truly felt and personally articulated responses to established literary work. 'Appreciation', Witkin wrote, 'needs not only to be relevant to the mental life of the child but it needs also to be integrated with his expressive activity'. In this continuous and developing relationship between expressive impulse, expressive medium and expressive symbolic form was seen to lie the common rhythm and preoccupation of all the arts in the curriculum. Informing the critique of English was a unified conception for aesthetic education. All the essential elements of art-making were present in English teaching, the project implied, but needed to be drawn down into a more creative and imaginative dynamic. The most ambitious aim of the project was to forge a language for understanding the way in which that dynamic worked in all the arts. Thus a debate was inaugurated which has become, over the last ten years, increasingly more urgent and more organized.

In 1982 the Gulbenkian foundation published its influential report *The Arts in Schools* and in 1983 the National Association for Education in the Arts was founded. Like the earlier Schools Council Project, *The Arts in Schools* report revealed a strong commitment to a unified conception of the arts:

> Our arguments in this report refer to all of the arts – music, dance, drama, poetry, literature, visual and plastic arts. We do not deal with them separately because we want to emphasize what they have in common – both in what they jointly offer education and in the problems they jointly face.[12]

The *Gulbenkian Report* offered a framework for an aesthetic education. The bold philosophical arguments derived from a central European tradition in aesthetics, going back through the work of Herbert Read and Louis Arnaud Reid, to Susanne Langer and Ernst Cassirer, to the philosophical work of Kant. The arts were seen to provide a unique and valuable kind of knowledge and thereby formed an indisputable part of any complete curriculum. The emphasis was on knowledge, but this aesthetic knowing was understood as materializing largely through the practice of art-making, through the pupil's direct engagement with the forms of art. What the report advocated was not so much the history or sociology of the arts as sustained practice with all kinds of expressive media. The educational distinctions should not be between cognition and affect, between thinking and feeling, but between different kinds of intelligence, different kinds of knowledge, different kinds of symbolic form. The task in the arts is to make objective the life of feeling and in so doing to bring sentience to conception and consciousness. In the words of the *Gulbenkian Report*:

> The arts are not outpourings of emotion. They are disciplined forms of inquiry and expression through which to organize feelings and ideas about experience. The need for young people to do this rather than just give vent to emotions or have them ignored, must be responded to in schools ...

> There are various kinds of thinking and various kinds of intelligence. None of them has a prior or self-evident right to dominate the others in the school curriculum. There is more than one mode of thought and action. Accordingly, there is more than one mode of creative thought, work and productivity and there are no grounds for the elevation of, for example, the sciences over the arts either in the policies or planning of the school curriculum. [13]

The notion of the arts – including literature and poetry – forming one symbolic community centrally concerned with a particular kind of knowing, a particular kind of creative intelligence, has dramatic and immediate implications for the English teacher. It was thus probably no historical accident, but rather a further manifestation of an emerging educational insight, that a year after the publication of the *Gulbenkian Report* the Association for the Verbal Arts published its manifesto and in Easter 1984 formally constituted itself under the chairmanship of Anne Cluysenaar. The aim of the Association was to foster the verbal arts and for its model of good practice it took the direct aesthetic approach of the other expressive disciplines. Their manifesto claimed:

> Urgent reforms are needed in the teaching of English, particularly in secondary schools and higher and further education. For most people, training in the verbal arts is a missing subject.

Other arts, such as music, painting, sculpture or drama, include practice as an essential component. In contrast, courses in literature usually concentrate on the understanding, description and evaluation of texts, with some attention to critical method ... This is an extraordinary situation.

It is an unfortunate anomaly that verbal arts as part of the discipline of classics were not carried over into the study of English when this became a major academic area in the early years of the century. It is time to return to a more effective and long established tradition. English, at all levels, should involve the study and practice of a wide range of modes, written and oral, literary and non–literary.

Too often, writing by children after they leave the primary school is unimaginative and unadventurous. What most second-ary school teachers are expected to ask from children is 'fair copy' work, safe writing with predictable and imposed subject matter. There are notable exceptions. Some teachers have achieved great success in developing imaginative writing, but they are in a minority. What is shown at 'O' level is reaped at 'A' level and beyond. Students of English at polytechnics and universities often write dull, secondhand discursive prose and do nothing else ... [14]

The manifesto went on to criticize the emphasis on free expression, the 'creative writing' condemned in the *Bullock Report*, and urged a concern for 'artistry in the handling of the medium' together with an awareness of the nature and history of the art-form; an emphasis all but identical to that of the *Gulbenkian Report*. What was more, the manifesto would seem to have united the English teaching community across the whole range of ideological commitment; it was, for example, signed by Brian Cox, by Richard Hoggart, David Holbrook, Ted Hughes, David Lodge and Raymond Williams. Was there an emerging consensus that the literary, practical and imaginative elements in English teaching had been neglected and that action was necessary to remedy the fault? The manifesto concluded:

Changes in the teaching of English are necessary and urgent if English is not only to survive the present difficult period but fulfil its promise as a major area of study and practice in the future. [15]

The message, it would seem, has not yet been heard by those formulating policies in English for the nation.

Some Conclusions

I want now to consider in turn the three major conceptions which I have historically delineated; first the conception of the relationship between language and learning; second, the conception of a thematic and project approach to literature; third, the conception of English as an aesthetic and creative discipline. With the HMI report at the centre of our attention I wish in the analysis to isolate the principles of an alternative conception of English.

The sociolinguist's concern to show the deep structural connections between language and learning was educationally sound. It had innumerable implications for all kinds of teaching across the whole range of symbolic forms. Mastering mathematics, mastering history, mastering geography, mastering science was seen to be, in large degree, a matter of mastering the particular kinds of discourse those disciplines require. Exactitude in description, the development of an argument, note-taking, critical reading of texts: these are irreducible tasks in the teaching of all the humanities and sciences. The principle at the heart of this issue was formulated in 1921, with both precision and passion, by George Sampson:

> Teachers seem to think that it is always some other person's work to look after English *But every teacher is a teacher of English because every teacher is a teacher in English*. That sentence should be written on letters of gold over every school doorway. Teachers are very specially the official guardians of the English language. We cannot give a lesson in any subject without helping or neglecting the English of our pupils. One of the most useful lessons in economy and lucidity of speech I have seen was actually a practical geometry lesson ...
>
> English reacts everywhere ...
>
> But let this be clear; no teachers whether of science, or languages, or mathematics, or history, or geography must be allowed to evade their own heavy responsibilities. They must not say 'Our business is to teach science or mathematics or French, not English'. That is the great fallacy of subject

teaching. It is very definitely their business to teach English; and their failure to recognize it as their business is a cause of the evil they deplore. In a sense the function of history, geography, science and so forth in school is to provide material for the teaching of English. The specialist teacher defeats his own purpose precisely to the extent to which he neglects the language of his pupils.[16]

The question raised by Sampson's insight and by the subsequent formulation in the *Bullock Report* of a language across the curriculum policy is this: if all teachers are teachers of language, what is the function of the English Department? If good teachers teach the linguistic skills that are inseparable from their own discipline of enquiry, why should these skills be taught again, outside a true context of learning, by the English teacher? In the HMI report *English from 5 to 16* the English Department is given responsibility for securing such objectives as:

Use writing to explore an issue and arrive at a conclusion.[17]

Record experiences and events accurately.[18]

Explain processes clearly.[19]

Frame instructions and directions clearly and succinctly.[20]

Expound an argument or thesis.[21]

Summarize the salient points of material heard or read.''

But all of these objectives are best developed as *an essential part of all the discursive disciplines*. Why, then, do they need to be duplicated in a context where they are in danger of becoming merely isolated skills? Indeed, in a school where there is an active language policy such practice seems educationally dangerous, in as much as it encourages a mechanistic view of skills disowned by the HMI themselves when they write: 'we must therefore assess (pupils') progress as people using language for the purposes necessary to people, not as mere language operators'.

At this point, another possibility opens up; namely, that English as a discipline is without coherence; that it exists, at best, merely to serve the needs of other autonomous enquiries or to cover instrumental skills not developed elsewhere (HMI specify the business letter and the *curriculum vitae*) or to be about 'communications' (but then what are the other disciplines doing if they are not communicating?). To counter such a disintegration, we must ask what *the distinctive field of enquiry* represented by the English teacher is. A coherent answer would be to say it is *literature, the making of literature and the appreciation and understanding of literature*. And if literature seems too vague a word, we can break it down into a series of genres called myth, story, novel, poetry, documentary, scripted drama etc., and these can be further broken down into sub-genres. The point is that there is a rich and unique symbolic field which if not represented by the English Department is thereby excluded from educational studies. The literary imagination is the centre of English; a centre which can be established in every school once a systematic language across the curriculum policy has been implemented, and the differentiation between English as a medium of learning and English as a symbolic field has been grasped. Many of the objectives listed by HMI will still pertain to English as a literary and expressive discipline (skill is always necessary, understanding of language crucial) but they will be seen as subordinate parts of a deeper and more coherent enterprise with its own distinctive aims and methods, but unrecorded by the HMI document. The condition for the realization of English as a literary-expressive discipline is, then, a language across the curriculum policy, the outcome of the sociolinguistic revolution we described at the beginning.

If literature, its creation (by pupils) and its understanding, is the core of English studies, then how are we to evaluate that ideological and thematic approach to literature delineated earlier in this chapter? The tendency to see literature as a means to discussion of social issues, while encouraging, often, a lively involvement of the pupils was in other respects something of a disaster. The fallacy of such an approach lies in the conception of literature as a series of discrete messages which can be unambiguously extracted from the form of the work and discussed in isolation from it. Literature does not have a transferable message; it *is* a meaning. That meaning cannot be adequately conveyed through a series of statements to be discussed; it is only grasped by engaging more and more precisely with the structural form of the work, with the actual syntactic energy, the actual metaphors, the actual narrative sequence. We come to understand the meanings of a work through imaginatively and sensuously coinciding with its formal energy. Thus the first movement in the teaching of literature should be to enter more and more adequately the poem or story or novel or myth, not to depart from it in a quick series of discursive leaps. (What is it about? What do you think about that view? When did you last ... argue with your parents?)

In the 1970s in many classrooms literature became badly reduced to thematic content. The range of literature became narrowed to fit the ruling assumption. Novels of a rather crude social realist kind became the inevitable fodder of thousands of adolescents. These were *not* seen as a particular form of genre which, like any other genre, abstracts and selects in terms of an artistic intention. They were seen to be, by implication, the heart of literature which was directly about life 'out there', to be instantly discussed in terms of politics, class, society. That such discussion has a place cannot be questioned; that it bypassed a prior aesthetic activity is what was invariably overlooked. Before works of art we are required to be co-artists. Seamus Heaney, writing about his own work, claimed 'the submerged intended paraphrasable content is not the immediate point, rather it is the lasciviousness of the language itself'. To miss that lasciviousness is to miss the embodied meaning of the poem. The approach of the 1970s was oddly out of tune with the spirit of literature. It held, at best, an inadequate naturalistic view of art; at worst, it merely abused literature to get to discursive discussion on a preordained theme. The imagination of Modernism rests on the primacy of the symbol, of the signifier over the signified. This, at a high critical level, has created a preoccupation with structure, with genre, with the formal possibilities of literature. It is time that this critical discussion began to inform the actual daily creative practice of English at primary and secondary level. The thematic approach to literature can now be seen to be simultaneously literal and reductive, promoting a discursive response long before aesthetic engagement had developed.

In brief, during the 1970s we discern a *complex movement, recorded at various levels of theory and practice, away from the sensitive and sustained teaching of literature.* The task now is not only to reclaim literature as the central ground of English teaching but also to establish more highly structured and sensitive methods for teaching it in intimate relationship with the imagination, creativity and feeling-life of our pupils.

David Allen in his *English Teaching Since 1965* adopted D.H. Lawrence's term 'art-speech' to make clear the distinctive nature of English teaching. He wrote:

Art-speech is not the only meaningful part of language, but it is a vital, living, part that is in danger of being mislaid, as one among many. It is the business of English to deal with that part; or to put it the other way round, there must be a place in the life of the school for art-speech and we might call that part English. [23]

The term 'art-speech' invites us, at once, to see the connections between English and all the other art disciplines. It encourages us to see that the aesthetic movement in arts education described earlier could have not a passing but a profound significance for the future of English teaching. As we have seen through the publication of the *Gulbenkian Report* and through the influence of the National Association for Education in the Arts, there has emerged a powerful argument for a unified aesthetic education in this country. The ambitious argument is attempting to establish, at least, three things:

(i)   a common language for understanding the arts in the curriculum;

(ii) a common practice which includes not only appreciation but also continuous practical experience in making and performing (within the community);

(iii) a common philosophy of art-making and art-responding which shows that the arts are concerned with a kind of meaning indispensable to education and the good society.

These claims further clarify the tasks of English. In fact, English teachers may well have a distinct contribution to make to the arts debate. After all, English teachers belong to a tradition which, since the time of Matthew Arnold, has struggled to locate the meaning and value of 'art speech' in the life of society. They belong to a tradition which at least since the time of Marjorie Hourd has included a classroom practice based upon a dialectic between critical appreciation and expressive activity. And during the last twenty years they have had, as we have seen, direct experience of reflecting on the nature of language, of forging language policies, of engendering language awareness. English teachers are thus in a unique position to contribute to that exacting struggle to fashion a common language for all the arts. At the same time, they would have an enormous amount to learn from a prolonged encounter with the other arts. They would be challenged to rethink much in their own teaching, their own methods of evaluation, their own examination systems. They would discover alternative models of learning, of practice, of performance, of assessment and find, frequently, unexpected vivifying points of contact and relationship. Their contribution, indeed, could become one vital part of a collaborative endeavour to create that unity between the divided art disciplines which would secure, for the first time in this country, an aesthetic education in our schools.

Here, then, in outline and in historical context, is our alternative conception of English. It is a radically different conception from that given in the HMI report; where their view is essentially eclectic, ours is essentially focal; where theirs is language-based, ours is based on a concept of a distinct discipline; where their view tends towards a notion of the transmission of diverse skills (tabulated in endless objectives) our emphasis, in contrast, is on a particular kind of knowing in relationship to a particular kind of symbolic form. However, it is essential to notice that English as an arts discipline is predicated upon a language across the curriculum policy – and that this policy described in and advocated by, The *Bullock Report*, explicitly covers most (for not all are equally sensible) of the objectives of the *English from 5 to 16* document. We have proposed the educational soundness of such a general approach. Such a policy gives English as a discipline a freedom to attend to the creative teaching of literature, that unique field of symbolic exploration not developed elsewhere in the curriculum. In this way we secure, at once, a sustained professional commitment to the language development of our pupils and a coherent education of the literary imagination. That such a literary-expressive education is aesthetic in kind and that it relates directly to all the other art disciplines has been one of the key propositions of this chapter. If the proposition has any power then it points English teachers to a further development; having disseminated language across the curriculum, English teachers should now contribute to the struggle to find a unifying language for the arts. It is, perhaps, here that the meaning and future of English lies? This, indeed, might secure the necessary conditions for the education of intellect and sensibility advocated by the HMI in their recent report on English.

Notes

1. Department of Education and Science (1984) *English from 5 to 16. Curriculum Matters I. An HMI Series*, DES, p. 22.
2. *Ibid.* p. 7
3. *Ibid.*
4. *Ibid.*
5. Department of Education and Science (1975) *A Language for Life (The Bullock Report)*, DES, pp. 188-98.
6. *Ibid.*, p. 163.
7. Department of Education and Science (1984) *op. cit.* p. 22.
8. *Ibid.*, p. 13.
9. *Ibid.*, p. 21.
10. ROSS, M. (1975) *Arts and the Adolescent: Schools Council Working Paper 54*. Evans/Methuen, pp. 47-8.

11. WITKIN, R. (1974) *The Intelligence of Feeling*, Heinemann Educational Books, pp. 38–9.
12. Calouste Gulbenkian Foundation (1982) *The Arts in Schools*, Calouste Gulbenkian Foundation, p. 10.
13. *Ibid.* p. 11 and p. 35.
14. Association for Verbal Arts (1983) *Manifesto* published in the *Times Higher Education Supplement*, 21 October.
15. *Ibid.*
16. SAMPSON, G. (1970) *English for the English*, Cambridge University Press, pp. 44–5.
17. Department of Education and Science (1984) *op. cit.* p. 11.
18. *Ibid.*
19. *Ibid.*
20. *Ibid.*
21. *Ibid.*
22. *Ibid.*, p. 12.
23. ALLEN, D. (1980) *English Teaching Since 1964*, Heinemann Educational Books, p. 102.

Chapter 4
The Aesthetic Field of English

Poetics must begin with genre.
                M.M. Bakhtin

Preamble

My aim in this chapter is to further delineate a formal aesthetics for the teaching of English. It is inevitable that I will cover some of the ground established in the last chapter, but my purpose here is more practical. It is to suggest the outlines of a programme for English studies, a programme based on aesthetic response to literature through the activities of appreciation, performance and expressive writing. Such a programme may not strike the reader as either radical or contentious, yet a practice based on a fundamental aesthetic premise hardly exists in this country, either at secondary or at university level. At the secondary level English has become insecure and impossibly diffused, running between 'skills', communications', 'comprehension exercises', 'mass media studies', 'linguistics' and 'literature'. At the university level English has splintered into a variety of movements, but most of them are centred on the ideological or historical analysis of 'texts', not on the development of aesthetic understanding and artistic production. Such a dominant academic practice represents, in large measure, 'the revenge of intellect on creativity' as Susan Sontag has eloquently phrased it. What is proposed in its place are ways of understanding which marry the literary medium, methods which keep close to the dynamic process of literary creation and aesthetic meaning. Such a position does not deny the need for analysis, theory and abstraction, but would have the general propositions and insights taken back into the aesthetic realm, to increase there the possibilities of creative action, of making, rendering and performing. Much of the emerging academic theory can serve aesthetic practice, but at the moment it tends rather arrogantly to usurp it. Part of the task, then, is to take current theory (and particularly structuralist theory) and reveal its dramatic implications for practical and artistic work in the teaching of English. However, before that is possible the present state of English as a discipline in the curriculum has to be encountered and resolved. It is here that I begin this detailed argument for an aesthetics of English.

The Diffused Eclecticism of English Studies

At the moment English as a discipline in the secondary curriculum has become amorphous, spread out and weakened by an excess of conflicting conceptual claims and by narrowing instrumental pressures. In any comprehensive school an English department may well be made up of a group of teachers who have radically different conceptions of their educational purposes; one member may see English as a 'service' department for other subjects; another may view it as concerned with 'communications'; another with the ideological reading of texts, another with the study of literature in an historical or aesthetic context; another with the development of the personality. Sometimes the differences are so marked, the conceptions and methods so disparate, that an English department comes to represent little more than a thinly disguised series of irreconcilable factions held together only by the external pressures of the examination system. In other cases, departments rush through a variety of approaches. A teacher of English, for example, describes her own experience working inside the same department of English:

> I've worked within a department which has moved from a thematic anti-textbook approach to a highly structured traditional approach ... to an experimental one-year integrated humanities course, to a reaffirmation of the place of literature as an integral part of English teaching; and finally and reluctantly to the realization that one approach isn't going to satisfy the needs of all the members of the department.[1]

The experience recorded here is indicative of the philosophical confusion. During the last ten years there has also been a widespread retreat to drab mechanical practices – the rote teaching of 'skills' isolated from actual contexts of productive learning – which, while seeming to conform to the external pressures exerted by government and industry, are without coherence and merely serve to compound further the educational and pedagogic chaos.

A diffused eclecticism of approach might, as the above writer suggests, seem the only pragmatic way forward, but such a position ducks the challenge of definition and debate, virtually allowing anything that happens in the English classroom, from grammatical box-analysis to solving crossword puzzles, to be the serious work of English teaching. In effect, such an eclectic position denies the conception of English as an autonomous discipline in the curriculum of human understanding. In this chapter it is precisely such a conception of symbolic autonomy which I aim to defend against general eclecticism and against the emergence of a notion of English as a kind of 'service' subject centrally designed to transmit instrumental skills.

Some of the problems which surround English in the curriculum derive from the word's double denotation; in educational contexts, English can mean either English as mother-tongue language (thus physics or sociology is learnt through *English*) or it can mean English as literature (thus one studies *English* at a university). One of the first premises of an autonomous conception of English in the secondary curriculum is that all teachers are teachers of English where it refers to the mother-tongue. This premise is far from new. It was formulated eloquently by George Sampson in 1920 and has, under the general impact of linguistics, been developed much more comprehensively during the last two decades, receiving a central place in The *Bullock Report* (1975). Such a premise means that the insights and conceptions deriving from, say, linguistics and semiotics, have a profound bearing on the teaching of the whole curriculum, affecting both the way we construe knowledge and meaning and the way we actually work in the classroom. The body of work developed largely inside English studies over the last twenty years around such notions as code, oracy, dialect, transactional-expressive-poetic forms of writing etc., thus impinge dramatically on all kinds of teaching and on all kinds of subjects. Furthermore it has become increasingly clear that to teach a subject is, to a significant degree, to teach the language of that subject. To teach history, for example, is to teach history-discourse. To teach history is to engender and make pertinent the categories of historical understanding; it is also to teach the various verbal procedures that the historical way of working requires or presupposes: the ability to cite relevant evidence, to make notes, to compose an argument, to question conclusions, to formulate other explanations. To teach history is to initiate pupils into that mode of discourse which renders the historian's way of reading experience. One of the major concerns of the historian is, then, to teach *the linguistic practices of the discipline*. What is true of history is, by extension, true of the other humanities and sciences.

This means that English, in the first sense, *of language*, must be a primary concern of all teachers. Such a notion gave birth to 'language across the curriculum'. It culminated in a number of important studies revealing the intimate reciprocal nature of language and learning and documenting the implications for the teaching of the sciences and the humanities.

The question arises as to the position of English teachers in this debate. It would seem axiomatic that an English department would have an important part to play in the formulation and execution of a language policy, fostering a general mother-tongue awareness and a *collective responsibility* for the development of pupils' language, fostering that initiation into those multiple discourses which constitutes the educational adventure, that initiation into formal techniques which makes it possible. But are its concerns exhausted here? Our answer to this question is 'No, not by any means'. For English has a distinctive symbolic field of its own to represent, namely English, in its second denotation, of *literature* or what we might call, more generally, *the literary mode of making, interpreting and understanding*. Here is the specific concern of English as a discipline not duplicated elsewhere in the curriculum. Put bluntly, if English teachers do not initiate their pupils into the field of literature (into the experience of making it, the experience of performing it, the experience of appreciating and absorbing it, of coming to understand it) it will not happen. One of the great symbolic ways of understanding will not be opened. A language across the curriculum policy disseminates a collective responsibility for language growth and, simultaneously, allows the English department to enter more decisively its own symbolic terrain. As a discipline its meaning and coherence lies in this terrain.

We come, then, to the question of teaching literature. On what principles should it be based? What approaches should be used? How should the work be developed? What connections with other disciplines, if any, should be forged? We come to the philosophy and practice of the teaching of English. Numerous conflicting answers can be provided. What follows is an attempt to delineate those which can be called 'the literary-expressive' or, alternatively, 'an aesthetic' or 'arts' approach. The emphasis falls not on the re-reading of literature as ideology, not on its analysis from a linguistic vantage-point, but on the envisagement of literature as an aesthetic field which to be entered requires, above all, the development of sensitive aesthetic response. This demands, as we shall see, virtually the reconstruction of English, the fashioning of a new model for its effective practice in our schools. It is to this model that I now wish to turn.

The Reconstruction of English as Art

English as a discipline aims to establish a vital and reciprocal connection between a developing awareness of literary work and the innate expressive propensity of the student. From this perspective, English most truly exists at the point of intersection between literary culture and the creative self. Thus the English teacher struggles to turn the classroom into a verbal crucible where what has been made in the culture, from Homer to Hughes, from Sappho to Anne Stevenson, is brought into the individual imagination and where what is created by the individual student is, in turn, brought into the culture through the communal life of the classroom, the school and the neighbourhood. This complex interaction between the innate expressive proclivity of the students' minds and the symbolic material of the culture creates the aesthetic field of English. Thus the approach is neither exactly symbol-centred nor child-centred, but exists essentially in that reciprocal movement between symbol and identity, in that formal and informal process of responding to and reconstructing the inherited store of myths, legends, stories, novels, poems, plays, the collective store of narrative and metaphor. English as an aesthetic practice lies in that labile space between what culturally exists and what has to be made existentially from it. It is vital to briefly consider the key word 'aesthetic' before moving on to outline the actual practice of such work.

By aesthetic I mean a particular way of responding to and organizing experience which is not abstract and propositional, but rather perceptual, concrete, and permeated with feeling. The aesthetic response resides in an intelligent perceptual feel for form, for the play between part and pattern, detail and *gestalt*. In the case of English it involves an imaginative – perceptual – bodily response to the qualities of language as they reveal themselves in action in, say, a particular story or poem. It involves a sensing of the texture of words, their individual tone, their cumulative rhythm, their imaginal energy, their multiple associations, their cluster of meanings. To develop the aesthetic is to develop an involvement with the expressive bodily life of language as it manifests itself in literature. In this context Virginia Woolf's manner of working comes to mind. According to E.M. Forster:

> She liked receiving sensations – sights, sounds, tastes – passing
> them through her mind, where they encountered theories and
> memories, and then bringing them out again, through a pen, on
> a bit of paper. Now began the higher delights of authorship. For
> these pen-marks on paper were only the prelude to writing,
> little more than marks on a wall. They had to be combined,
> arranged, emphasized here, eliminated there, new relationships
> had to be generated, new pen-marks born, until out of the
> interactions, something, one thing, one, arose. This one thing,
> whether it was a novel or an essay or a short story or a
> biography or a private paper to be read to her friends, was, if it
> was successful, itself analogous to a sensation. Although it was
> so complex and intellectual, although it might be large and
> heavy with facts, it was akin to the very simple things which
> had started it off, to the sights, sounds, tastes. It could be best
> described as we describe them. For it was not about something.
> It was something.[2]

To be understood by her reader that 'something' must, in turn, be
experienced as a kind of complex sensation resonant with meaning. The
organization of the work manifests to the reader, sensitive to the diverse
impressions created by its specific use of language, its multiple meanings. Only in and through such an aesthetic response can the many
interior meanings of art be grasped. Yet so many approaches to
literature tend to bypass this primary action of engaging with the work.
There has been a marked tendency in schools to use only social realist
literature and to assume that literature is exclusively 'about' things
which once conceptually located simply require discursive consideration. Literature, in brief, has been raided for 'material' for discursive
purposes: material on social class, on the family, on sex, on indus-
trialism. The novel and story have been used as a means to reach liberal
debate or to act as a mere trigger to start some general project which
soon swallows and forgets its starting stimulus, whether it be Charles
Dickens or George Eliot, Shakespeare or Sylvia Plath. At some
universities, too, the prevailing practice has come to regard literary
work as ideological constructs (often masked, and, therefore, in need of
deconstruction) to be evaluated through sociological categories (generally Feminist or Marxist in kind). In both cases – in the secondary
classroom, in the university lecture theatre – analytical attention with
an extractable content has made irrelevant the demanding act of first

engaging with the art *as art*. Such a literalization of literature calls for its liberation, its return to the aesthetic field in a context of active reading, active performance, practical experimentation. We need to re-establish a fitting relationship with the actual medium we are studying if we are to know its nature and be developed by contact with it. We need to evolve poetic ways to understand poetry; literary ways to understand literature; mythical ways to understand myth; imagistic ways to understand image. Here analytical work and discursive understanding may serve an essential function, but their conclusions need to be taken back down into the primary realm of aesthetic engagement. The truths of abstract reflection need to be taken back into the life of the senses and of the imagination, need to be taken down into the creative unconscious and reconstituted as art. The theory needs to be translated into an artistic grammar to expand the possibilities of aesthetic practice. Taking the notion of genre I would like to outline one possibility.

The Centrality of Genre

One way of developing English as an aesthetic discipline is through the notion of genre, a notion which has received new intellectual life in the writings of the Russian Formalists, the French Structuralists and such influential critics as Northrop Frye. The study of genre provides an understanding of the formal possibilities of expressive utterance. It opens up the field of literary studies, indicates its true scope and provides a variety of models for appreciation and creative imitation. The creative application of genre to English studies could generate a more comprehensive and a richer practice. If the conception of English as a subject concerned essentially with literature appears to narrow it, then the notion of genre immediately expands it – for literature is a universe made up of many symbolic galaxies, all of which require attention and recognition. The differentiation of types helps us to define an appropriate syllabus.

A crude working list of literary genres can be given as follows:

> Poetry
> Myth
> Fairy tale
> Novel
> Story
> Autobiography
> Journal/diary

Letter
Memoir
Documentary
Scripted drama
Essay and Sketch
Rhetoric (public speech, polemic, etc.)

Each of these genres requires further definition and qualification, but this is not the place for such detailed analysis. Certainly the list is not definitive. It is intended only to indicate the range of literary types the discipline of English should be concerned with. The enumeration of the genres enables us to see what has been excluded. How many English students regularly study or make documentaries? How many engage systematically with myths and fairy stories? How many really work the field of autobiography or memoir?

Furthermore, each genre can be effectively broken down into a variety of species which, while distinctive, yet possess certain structural elements which make them members of the same class. To consider the species of each genre is to locate precisely the formal conventions of literature; to locate the conventions is to provide the means for further recreation and experimentation; it is to give the grammar of aesthetic production. As one example I would like to take the genre of the novel/story and develop a list of modes based on the techniques through which the narrative can be constructed; the nine ways of telling a tale. Here, then, is a working list of the narrative modes:

Epistolary
Journal/diary
Documentary
Dialogue
First person narration
Second person narration
Third person narration
Stream of consciousness
Experimental

Once again my purpose is not to elaborate on all of these modes, although in Chapter 8 I will consider the genre of autobiography in some detail. In practice most novels are, of course, mixed. I list them so as to draw attention to the complexity of the symbolic field, to the multiplicity of conventions used by the story tellers, to the techniques which have to be appropriated for the telling of stories to continue at a level which corresponds to contemporary consciousness. Of course, they need to be introduced not as dead schema but *the actual means for the embodiment of living and imaginative experience*. How can this notion of genre be put to aesthetic use?

Virgina Woolf wrote:

> Perhaps the quickest way to understand the element of what a novelist is doing is not to read but to write, to make your own experiment with the danger and difficulty of words.[3]

To this one would also add the need to actively experiment with different formal constructions: the use of the journal (as in, for example, *Adrian Mole, The Diary of Ann Frank, Blindness*); the use of the first person (as in *Huckleberry Finn, David Copperfield, Robinson Crusoe*); the use of letters (as in *A Bundle of Letters, Humphrey Clinker* and *The Colour Purple*) etc. Such experimentation could take a number of directions. The teacher, for example, could take into a class a traditional third-person narrative story like Stan Barstow's *The Fury* and, after responding to it as a complete story, work on its latent narrative possibilities by asking the students: (a) to develop, using the story's conventions, an alternative ending; (b) to take a minor character and still in the style of the story tell his or her story. Alternatively one could move to the other narrative modes and, for example (c) take Mrs. Fletcher when she smashes the vase and render her state of mind through the inner monologue 'stream of consciousness' technique; or (d) take two characters and bring them into narrative contact through a written exchange of letters. What we are doing in such work is fostering an awareness of convention, developing expressive and imaginative powers, working literature within its own medium. If we consider all the genres and their species, the way they are separate from each other and the way they are interdependent (the mode of autobiography suggesting a plausible mode for fiction, the mode of fiction in turn suggesting another form for autobiography, etc.) we can see that the symbolic field of English is, in principle, indescribably rich. The critic, Julia Kristeva has written:

> every text takes shape as a mosiac of citations, every text is the absorption and transformation of other texts. The notion of intertextuality comes to take the place of intersubjectivity.[4]

The aim of English as an aesthetic and productive discipline is to place the student in the centre of that intertextuality, to make him or her a reader, a writer, a performer, a producer at the heart of the cultural process. A sensitive application of the genres to reading and writing is one way of achieving this. The enumeration of the genres might also possess a value in providing a principle for the organization of a comprehensive English syllabus. Here my aim is merely to describe a few of the possibilities such analysis releases.

Performance as Interpretation

Another way of developing English as an arts discipline is through performance. *Performance is critical interpretation kept within the medium of the art-work.* Paul Valery claimed of poetry that it had 'no existence at all ... It comes to life only in two situations – in the state of composition in a mind that nominates and constructs it, and in the state of recitation.' The remark suggests a method which needs in the teaching of English to be developed further. The oral rendering of texts requires the development of those qualities an actor brings to a script, an attention to all the specificities of the work as they unite to create a compelling aesthetic *gestalt*. Such work links poetry to the power of speech and to the power of aural imagination. Like a scripted play the poem (or story or myth) has to be lifted off the page and given a physical life, a life which depends upon the breath, the pulse of blood, the movement of the throat, lips and tongue, which possesses the animation of the spoken word. Done well such work ensures that responses are rooted in the aesthetic and perceptual mode and that the mind's attention is given to the nature of the art-work itself.

There is much to be done here. Yet our inherited traditions of critical and discursive work conspire against it. What is needed is suggested more by the workshop where actors and actresses prepare for rehearsals, than by the academic seminar or the ordinary classroom. A recent tape *The Sound of Poetry* signposts a way forward and offers a practical development. In their introductory pamphlet Edwin Webb and Edward Lee write:

> ... the overwhelming tradition of poetry in English is not 'visualist'. 'The look of the thing' may be important – but except in those poems which are really an extension of graphics, layout and structure are means towards the end of its aural perception. For this major tradition of poetry is founded on a form of speech-making – whatever degree of formality or informality is assumed in the speech-mode: whether intimate confession, conversation or public rhetoric. Thus attending to

how one would actually say the speech yields quite naturally
certain realisations of the language. It leads us to *hear* what we
might *overlook*. The purpose of the tape is therefore, quite
simply, to encourage students of poetry to *say* the poem: to
experiment actively with ways of making the sound of the
speech contained in the poem. In that improvisation ('How
might this sound?' or 'How would one say that?') students will
be encouraged to explore the resources of oral language and
thus be engaged in the *production* of meaning.[5]

With this kind of oral/aural attention the work on the poem ceases to be
'an exercise in the comprehension of print symbols' and becomes an
aesthetic exercise in the recreation of poetic meanings. There is an
analogy with music (one thinks, inevitably, of T.S. Eliot's *Four Quartets*
and *Preludes*). The poem can be envisaged as a musical score which
comes to life in its actual rendering when the sounds are recreated
through the interpretive powers of the reader–conductor and the
listening audience. As a work of music can have many different
renderings so can a work of poetry. We could say that *the poem has as
many meanings as the voice can render with artistic effect.* Here is a form of
deconstruction within the aesthetic practice of English! Of course, not
all poems need reading aloud but it is important to note that even silent
reading requires an internalization of *sounding the words and hearing them
in the auditory imagination.* If that does not take place the poem as a poem
cannot be experienced. We are left with the unsettling question as to
how many in our culture know how to read poetry silently, never
having heard it rendered with intelligence and power. The invention of
the cassette has made possible the most careful work in this neglected
area of English. Such renderings of literature could form an essential
part of the aesthetic practice of English teaching. Indeed, finding one's
own 'voice' in the 'voices' of others acts as a metaphor for the nature of
the whole enterprise.

The Dynamic Nature of the Process

I have suggested throughout that students of English must be seen as
makers, as individuals who have an innate expressive need to explore
their experience and the experience of their culture through their own
creative acts. They need to know the grammar of literature partly so
that, at varying levels, they can create their own literature. This means

TAILPIECE TO *IN PARENTHESIS*: THE VICTIM

Plate 12   David Jones tailpiece to In Parenthesis.
The formal appreciation of David Jones requires a visual arts understanding as much as a literary one.

that we urge them to keep note-books recording stray images, conversational fragments, resonant quotations, observations, speculations. We urge them to actively experiment with the various genres and their innumerable modes: experimenting with the making of documentaries, with the making of autobiographies, with the making of ballads and haikus, with the making of traditional and experimental stories, with the making of contemporary fairy-tales and myths. We urge them to work through drafts, to revise, to edit, to adapt in order to achieve the finished artefact. We urge that the finished art-work be, in some way, performed or published or displayed so that it invites from others aesthetic response as well as critical and appreciative commentary. Here students need to become aware of the dynamics of the creative act, the stages of the writing process. Through the examination of the working drafts of poems by, say, Yeats or Wilfred Owen, students can see the labour or making in which the cliché can be redeemed and the vague abstraction made palpable. Part of the work of the English department, we could say, is *production*; the production of anthologies, of reviews, of plays, of readings on cassettes, of autobiographies, stories and myths;

the continuous creation of a body of work to be experienced by the class, the school and the community.

Conclusion

Such a reformulation of English points it towards all the other expressive arts; dance, mime, music, drama, art, film. Yet while the many connections become only too visible at a conceptual level, at a practical level most of them still remain to be forged. The past and current practice of English has lead in other directions, towards the humanities and particularly towards linguistics (of the *Language in Use* kind). Yet if we consider the genres again as the means for demarcating our symbolic concerns, the connections with the other arts become quickly clear. Many forms of poetry belong with music (the ballad, the song, the incantation); some belong with the visual arts (kinetic poetry typographical poetry, poster poetry). A consideration of the documentary soon leads to theatre, to film, to radio and photography. Autobiography has its correspondence in the visual arts in the self-portrait and

Plate 13   From William Blake's The Marriage of Heaven and Hell.
In William Blake image and text work together to create a single aesthetic unity.

vital connections in our century with photography, while myth moves across to dance and drama. Even in a more restricted kind of study the formal appreciation of such writers as William Blake, William Morris, David Jones requires a visual arts understanding as much as a literary one, while the appreciation of Shakespeare or Beckett requires a knowledge of both literary and theatrical practice. The connections are *there* in the aesthetic works but have been overlooked because English has been conceived as an analytical subject belonging to the humanities, rather than one belonging with the other arts.

Once English has been reconstituted as an arts discipline (while keeping necessary connection with the humanities and indeed, with the whole curriculum through a coherent language policy) then two further questions follow: Where does English belong in the larger family of the arts? And how can this position best be represented and organized within the narrow constraints of the National Curriculum? These two questions are of and for the future. Here my aim has been to outline some of the elements in the initial reconstruction of English as art.

Notes

1. Yvonne Horton in an unpublished essay for the MA course Language, Arts and Education at the University of Sussex, Spring term 1983.
2. FORSTER, E.M. on Virginia Woolf in (1965) *Two Cheers for Democracy*, Penguin, p. 250.
3. WOOLF, V. (1932) *The Second Common Reader*, Hogarth Press, p. 259.
4. KRISTEVA, J. (1973) quoted in CULLER, J. *Structuralist Poetics*. Routledge and Kegan Paul, pp. 139–40.
5. WEBB, E. and LEE, E. (1982) in a pamphlet accompanying *The Sound of Poetry*, Sussex Tapes.

Chapter 5
Art and the Loss of Art in an Age of Spilt Science: The Demise of Late Modernism

Art is the creation of forms symbolic of human feeling...The making of this expressive form is the creative process that enlists a man's utmost technical skill in the service of his utmost conceptual power, imagination. Not the invention of new original turns, nor the adoption of novel themes, merits the word 'creative', but the making of any work symbolic of feeling, even in the most canonical context and manner.

Susanne Langer

The notion of the avant-garde is intimately related to that of progress; it implies that art progresses along with society, technology, etc. Very few artists today cling to this consolation. The beatific faith in human perfectability leads us to the great nightmares of our times.

Carlos Fuentes

Preamble

Throughout the last chapters I have implicitly and explicitly been critical of Modernism but not fully explained my reasons for the opposition. It is time to do so. Much of what is to follow was written for a Welsh Arts Council Conference held in 1979. In the years since that Conference there has been a discernible shift in the education and arts world. In 1979 it seemed as if one were attacking Late Modernist art from a position of extreme isolation and vulnerability against something which had all the appearance of being permanently established. Now, writing in 1988, it looks as though the blind, limping creature of Late Modernism has become more and more recognized for the sick invalid it had become. I do not think the Conference was responsible for the change! But I do think that what two of us argued before the Arts Council was somewhat in advance of a deep aesthetic change now taking place. Because of our contribution to the Conference I have been interested to note some of the subsequent occasions in which trenchant criticism of the contemporary visual arts broke through the silence to be recorded in influential places. I will confine myself in this preamble to three quotations.

On 20 November 1980, under the title 'In the end, even shock becomes a bore', Roy Strong reviewed a new book on modern art by Norbert Lynton. Strong wrote against what he called 'the modern art industry':

> I'm resentful of its patronizing attitude to artists whom it banishes beyond the pale – Sutherland or Ivon Hitchens don't even figure; I'm irritated by its pretensions; I groan at its often unnecessary aggressiveness; and I'm often affronted by the downright poor workmanship and shoddy technique which its exponents sometimes outrageously flaunt. The public has been brainwashed by decades of the modern art machine, a complex mechanism whose interests lie in sustaining the myth of modern art. As a result, we are saddled with something which is the consequence of tremendous vested interests by both the people and the institutions whose existence could be undermined if they admitted it was now a myth. After all, if you are a director of a museum of modern art, it is unlikely that you would ever want to upset the notion. This is a problem that has never bedevilled the creation of art before in quite the same way. It will be interesting to know what, in a century's time, will be made of this huge monster made up of museums, critics, journals, salerooms and dealers dedicated to the instant recognition and propagation of modern art. [1]

Such direct speaking on the visual arts in *The Listener* at that time amounted almost to a revolution. The avant-garde were meant to be, by journalist definition, the creative élite or, at least, trendsetters.

I have another cutting which comes not from *The Listener* but from *The Sunday Times* for the same month but a year later. One should not expect much beyond modish euphoria in the 'quality' Sunday papers, but here in November 1981 was a reviewer writing on John Russell's *The Meanings of Modern Art* and describing 'the terror of being branded as out of date if one damns or even if one fails to embrace the "latest development"'. The reviewer, Nicholas Perry, went on to claim:

> This has paralysed the traditionally polemical character of art
> journalism and encouraged the avoidance of negative evalua-
> tions generally in art criticism. Revised estimates of the merits
> of modern art are also obviously against the interests of the
> public institutions which have, as never before, 'invested' in it.
> But the reputation of modern artists have been created by a
> specialist section of the art-loving public – by a far smaller
> proportion of that public than in any former century – and
> they are bound to be challenged. The sooner this happens the
> better ...[2]

One had to rub one's eyes and read again. These subversive truths
were actually being expressed in *The Sunday Times* amid the platitudes,
the cleverness, the modishness.

Some time later in the autumn of 1982 I came across an essay by the
English art-critic Peter Fuller published in the Australian journal *The
Age* in which he argued that contemporary art had, in large measure,
betrayed the aesthetic dimension (in which transcendence is possible) by
submitting itself to the reality principle. 'Modern art', wrote Fuller,
'relinquished creativity in the name of the object.' The essay was,
significantly, entitled *Crisis in the Arts* and began as follows:

> A spectre is haunting Europe, America, and no doubt these
> antipodes, too. the spectre of Post-Modernism. Western culture
> is undergoing a transforming shift in its 'structure of feeling'.
> But perhaps the image of a revolution in taste is wrong, because
> what is occurring in aesthetic life today is recuperative, and, in
> many ways, profoundly conservative. Of course, this aesthetic
> conservatism cannot be equated with the mood of political
> conservatism that is infecting Western societies; indeed it may
> have more in common with say the 'progressive' conserva-
> tionism of the ecological lobby, or the anti-nuclear movements,
> than with anything that might comfort, Reagan, Thatcher or
> Malcolm Fraser.
>
> When I set out as a professional critic in the late 1960s, the
> history of recent art was still presented as an ever-evolving
> continuum of mainstream fashions. Museums, magazines and
> books encouraged the view that Abstract Expressionism gave
> way to Post-Painterly Abstraction and Pop, which were
> followed by Minimalism and photo-Realism which, in turn,

inevitably gave way to such non-painterly activities as Conceptualism, 'mixed media', photo-text, Theoretical Art, and so on. Thus in the early 1970s, the assertion of 'The Death of Painting' had become a commonplace of 'progressive' taste. Art students, for example, seemed preoccupied with the arrow of the so-called 'avant-garde' as it sped on down a narrowing tunnel in which more and more of the painter's traditional concerns were shed.

Last year, however, a massive exhibition at the Royal Academy, London, heralded 'A New Spirit in Painting': a 'turning back to traditional concerns'.[3]

The three examples are merely intended to illustrate an extraordinary creative change in understanding. This is still dramatically manifesting itself in our culture in all the art disciplines but perhaps most obviously in architecture. In the light of these changes I could have rewritten my Conference paper, made it less rough, more in tune, but I would rather it remain as it was written in 1979. I leave it without a change. The reader will be able to recognize its intimate relationship with the other chapters in this volume and in particular with the symposium *Living Powers: The Arts in Education* which was built

Claes Oldenburg

Plate 14   Claes Oldenburg I ardines (undated).
Late Modernist art lured into a false framework of reference betrayed the very principles of expressive aesthetic activity.

uncompromisingly on the premise first established in this paper, namely that Late Modernism was over and that now the challenge was to find or rather *reclaim* a much more comprehensive ground for the effective and sustained teaching of all the arts.

If Chapter 2 offered some of the tenets for a reconstruction of the arts, then this chapter (read in conjuction with Chapter 9) offers a critique of quite recent practice, with its focus strongly on the visual arts.

Paper given at the 1979 Welsh Arts Council Conference: Creativity and Deception, based on Giles Auty's book 'The Art of Self Deception'

Introduction

In this paper I have set myself two aims. The first one is to briefly delineate the emerging literature of protest against most of the dominant trends in contemporary art. The second is to develop these criticisms into a broader philosophical argument. In the main part of the paper I want to suggest that to a large degree contemporary art has been lured into a false framework of reference and understanding, with the result that it has betrayed the very principles of expressive aesthetic activity. Paradoxically, art has turned against itself and, in a suicidal fit, come near to destroying its own nature. It is the aim of this paper to try and understand why this suicide has taken place. Before developing my own philosophical argument, however, I would like to refer to some of the literature, mostly ignored by the art establishment, which has drawn attention to the present crisis in the visual arts.

The Emerging Literature of Protest

Herbert Read, who spent a considerable amount of his time and intellectual energy championing new movements, felt towards the end of his life that many 'progressive' developments had not only become excessive but were, under the name of art, destroying the very nature of art. In *The Limits of Permissiveness*, a lecture given four months before his death in June 1968 and printed in *The Black Rainbow: Essays on the Present Breakdown of Culture*, Heinemann Educational Books, 1975, Herbert Read defended the *principle of modernism* which he called 'the principle of symbolism as distinct from the principle of realism', but attacked movements like Action Painting, Pop and Op Art. He claimed they were pseudo-movements with labels conferred by publicity men and journalists:

> The so-called movements that have followed (the last surrealist movement of 1947) – Action Painting in the United States, Pop Art and Op Art – have been pseudo-movements without stylistic unity, without manifestoes, without common action or association of any kind – the creation of journalists, anxious, to find a label for phenomena they do not understand, even anxious to create an order where only confusion seems to exist.[4]

Herbert Read also attacked 'contemporary nihilism' and claimed that the critic had to withhold his approval from all those manifestations of permissiveness 'characterized by incoherence, insensibility, brutality and ironic detachment'. *The Limits of Permissiveness* remains an important essay, a defence of the principle of true art against all the fashionable distortions which have become associated with it.

If Herbert Read pointed to some of the pathologies of contemporary art, Lewis Mumford (1971) in *The Pentagon of Power* (Secker and Warburg) gave them a historical analysis, seeing them as the symptoms of a civilization driven forward by a belief in mechanism, measurement, and mass-production. *The Pentagon of Power* is a sustained analysis of the mechanical world-picture which has its roots in the philosophical and scientific thinking of the Renaissance. Part of the book relates the state of modern culture, with its inveterate tendency to deny the historical and cultural, to the informing belief in technology which drives our society 'forwards' (hence the belief in Progress). The arts, in many cases, serve only to reinforce the impersonal dictates of the machine. Mumford writes:

> In every country today, a large part of the population, literate or subliterate, indoctrinated by the mass media, reinforced by the more fashionable leaders in schools, colleges, and museums, accepts this madhouse 'art', not only as a valid expression of our meaningless and purposeless life – as in one sense it actually is – but as the only acceptable existential approach to reality. Unfortunately, the effect of this publicity and indoctrination is to intensify the underlying irrationality of the power system, by eliminating every possible reminder of those cumulative human traditions which, energetically recultivated and renewed, are still needed to transform it.[5]

The power of Mumford's work resides in its historical understanding, its breadth of vision, its ability to see in the seemingly isolated and trivial event, general ideological currents and the great uncertain movements of human consciousness. The analysis which I will develop later in this lecture will not be significantly different, I think, from that of Mumford.

Tom Wolfe's polemic on contemporary art, *The Painted Word*, was published in America in 1975 and was published in this country as a long article in *Harpers and Queen* (February 1976). It is a word-drunk piece of writing – the publishers, with their unerring power to pull up a flattering word, call it 'incandescent'. It lacks profundity and avoids definitions, yet nevertheless it serves a purpose by documenting the way in which art can be packaged and made to sell. Wolfe gives us firm evidence for Herbert Read's assertion that Action painting was a pseudo-movement. The description of the rise of Jackson Pollock is worth quoting in some detail:

> Greenberg didn't discover Pollock or even create his reputation, as was said so often later. Damnable Uptown did that. *Pick me!* Peggy Guggenheim picked Pollock. He was a nameless down-and-out hobo Cubist. She was the niece of Solomon (Guggenheim Museum) Guggenheim and the centre of the most chic uptown art circle in New York in the 1940s ... In a single year, 1943, Peggy Guggenheim met Pollock, gave him a monthly stipend, got him moving in the direction of surrealist automatic writing, set him up on Fifty-Seventh Street with his first show ... got Sweeney to write the catalogue introduction, in prose that ranged from merely rosy to deep purple dreams – and Barr inducted one of the paintings, the She Wolf, into the Museum of Modern Art's Permanent Collection – and Motherwell wrote a rave for Partisan Review – and Greenberg wrote a super-rave for *The Nation* ... The Consummation was complete and Pollock was a success before the last painting was hung and the doors were opened and the first Manhattan was poured on opening night.[6]

Four people with money, power over galleries, and contact with the media, and a reputation can be made! '*And Pollock was a success before the last painting was hung!*' The painter does not become famous. He is made famous. And just as he is turned from painter into personality, so is his art turned into fashion, and soon after advertising imagery. Wolfe's book has a certain value in exposing the mechanisms of this manufacturing process.

In 1977 two further books were published in this country. Marion Boyars brought out a translation of Helene Parmelin's *Art Anti-Art* and Libertarian Books brought out Giles Auty's *The Art of Self-Deception*. Helene Parmelin's book is rather opaque and badly written. The argument digresses more than it progresses. But it does confirm, with examples taken from Paris, our general analysis of the state of the visual arts and some of these examples I will employ later in my own argument. It also makes a useful distinction between Design (Op and Pop) and Art (the unique interpretation and presentation of experience through symbolic form). Giles Auty's book is, in every respect, superior. He writes as an artist who refuses to meet the required formulae. He writes, therefore, with a compelling urgency and with examples drawn straight from his own experience. In fact, the book provides an excellent critical introduction to the contemporary art-world in England. The author analyzes with considerable care the many fallacies which inform modish discussion about the arts. Perhaps the greatest fallacy of all derives from an unquestioned belief in inevitable progress, i.e. that whatever comes next must be better than what preceded it. As I will argue more fully later, applied to the arts such an assumption creates havoc. It provides a simple justification for endless gimmickry and perpetual change (whatever its worth).

In an autobiographical passage Giles Auty describes how looking at a Velazquez in the Prado, Madrid, he suddenly saw through the false notion of time which informs technological civilization. It is an eloquent passage and conveys a major insight into the dilemma of the contemporary arts:

> What I 'saw' in that moment would be hard to define exactly. Perhaps, more than anything, that it was essential for the painter to possess a broader and more Godlike view of time – for the three hundred odd years since Velazquez painted his triumphant *Las Meninas* was, in reality, but an eye's wink distant; that for a painter a binding sense of the present was simply a prison; that time as commonly portrayed by modern art historians had neither artistic validity nor sense.
>
> The truly staggering gap between the quality of work by Velazquez ... and of all contemporary painting with which I was then familiar, lay not only in technique but, at least equally, in philosophy and spirit. Our much-acclaimed artistic progress and evolution were not sky or upward-bound as the authorities had tried to tell us, but sharply downward in every artistic sense that mattered.[7]

Giles Auty is here personally testifying to that return to cumulative human traditions which Lewis Mumford advocates. However, it is crucial that, in returning to sources and in discovering much needed continuities, the best of the modern – the very great achievement of Henry Moore, Picasso, and Klee, for example – is in no way neglected or denied. There are moments when the author seems in danger of excluding great forms whose inspiration derives from within the psyche (within dream, memory, and archetype) rather than from without. This is a pity because in attacking the false and the merely modish it is important that comprehensive principles, rather than schools, are established. The battle is not between figurative and non-figurative but between art and non-art. However, as I have said, the book is valuable, its criticism of the art establishment both trenchant and accurate and its belief in the humanity and vision of the great painter badly needed.

A further attack on theoretical art and the Tate Gallery's bias in that direction was made by David Hockney in *The Observer* (4 March 1979). Most of what Hockney said had been argued rather more adequately by Giles Auty but it is nevertheless good to see such incisive criticism given proper space in a weekly newspaper. The numerous letters which were published two weeks later gave unambiguous expression to a tremendous dissatisfaction with the state of the arts and, in particular, the Tate Gallery's absurd purchases, not only the purchase of Carl Andre's *Equivalent VIII* but also such other non-art as, for example, Joseph Beuy's *Fat Battery*, Marcel Broadthaer's *Casserole and Closed Mussels* and Keith Arnatt's *Self Burial*.

The literature of protest, scattered and uneven as it is, would have us critically question the 'art' so endlessly paraded by the art-critics, art-dealers and art-bureaucrats of our time.

Art in the Shadow of Science

I want now to draw the various criticisms of contemporary art into a unified intellectual framework. It seems to me that art and expression are suffering from a major confusion of categories. In Western civilization there has been for at least the last 300 years a marked tendency to reduce the various symbolic dimensions of the human mind to one dimension, namely that of the mathematico-scientific. The consequences of this reduction are visible today in every activity of man, but are revealed most dramatically of all in architecture and the visual arts.

The impersonal tower blocks of steel and glass in cities, the minimal surfaces of many contemporary canvases, the widespread cerebralism (expressed, for example, in Norbert Lynton's 'all art is a form of applied thought'), the arid reproduction of mass-produced artefacts like tins of soups and coca-cola bottles in pop art, all testify to a deep failure of the mind to engage passionately, imaginatively, and meaningfully with experience. All these art forms would seem to offer the artist a psychological protection against the fullness of his own existence; they provide conventions which positively allow the artist, in fact, to avoid a confrontation with the depths of his own being. My contention is that far from being revolutionary, most contemporary forms of art demand a conformity and comparative superficiality of mind. It would seem that the student of a typical art college in this country does not have his mind opened to the range of human emotion and the creative task of personal expression; he is, rather, encouraged to restrict the range of his consciousness and to master a set of fashionable and enclosing mannerisms. There is a danger that he absorbs two poisonous messages: the first is technicism, the second is an adaptive cynicism.

By technicism I refer to that notion that art is a specialism concerned primarily with solving its own technical problems without any reference to the compelling urgencies of life. In the current jargon art becomes a specialized form of 'problem-solving', or to quote an even more extreme statement of David Thompson of *Studio International*, 'art is as much a specialised discipline as nuclear physics'. Such a technicism robs art of its humanity and universality. In my view there could not be a more corrosive formula to hand to a rising generation of artists. The second notion I have called 'adaptive cynicism'. Here the emphasis is on relevance, reflection of the modern world, the immediate reproduction of whatever seems dominant in the industrial and commercial environment. The notion is not: 'these are the experiences and cultural forms now confronting humanity. Let us see what they mean, both what they portend and what lies beneath them.' It is not explorative or interpretative. It is static and reproductive. The implication is: 'These things are real for contemporary society, therefore they should be the real objects in your art.' Invariably under such a rubric, art becomes an extension of pop culture; celebrating the same values, instant success, momentary fun, endless chop and change, brashness, casualness of style. Art becomes ephemera, an ephemera which is absurdly grotesquely inflated and fossilized when it is purchased and hung up in museums and art galleries, a fossilization which, significantly, we have not heard pop-artists complaining about. *What is so*

87

inadequate about pop-art is its intrinsic conservatism. Instead of questioning or illuminating contemporary experience, it merely conserves it in the most static manner. Pop-art locks us into the status quo and like the status quo it negates our potential humanity. Like advertising, on which it parasitically draws, it persuades us to accept ourselves as less than human and is not even aware of the fact. In *Pop as Art* Mario Amaya wrote:

> Such artists accept the despicable with a terrible *sang-froid*, and in a way that implies they are neither hating nor loving, but just having. Instead of taking up the fight against mass-thinking, they have reflected it, parrot-like in their own works, over and over again ...[8]

Precisely! They embody and disseminate an adaptive cynicism, a mode of experiencing the world which is deeply defensive, settling for the stereotype rather than the pain and delight of authentic experience. In fact, both technicism and adaptive cynicism have this in common: they are defences against the existential tasks of living. They are closed against the slow growth of the artist's experience through the passionate refinement of symbolic form. In both cases, they cut off before the real challenges of life and art have been confronted. Mr. Adams in his paper declared that the artist had to be ready to take risks but there are no existential risks taken in the sort of 'art' he is so willing to defend.

Technicism and *adaptive cynicism.* I have selected two powerful notions which would seem to be damagingly at work in the contemporary art-world. As I have suggested, they are not unrelated, for both conspire to deny the disturbing/enriching/moving human dimension of art. They see art technically or literally but never as the symbolization of personal vision. Yet they remain highly representative of the sort of understanding which now unifies much of the work done in art colleges, the work selected for exhibitions, the way those exhibitions are reviewed, the way the Arts Council distributes its cash etc., etc. How are we to understand this complex pattern of reference and assumption which now tenuously holds the art-world together? Obviously it would be possible for an art-critic to show how current movements have evolved by their own logic from previous traditions, to relate aesthetically contemporary work to, say, the Bauhaus or the Dadaists. I am in no way equipped to offer such an analysis. I want to offer a broader interpretation; I want to suggest that whatever movements in contemporary art may have developed from earlier movements, they have nearly all been deeply, if unconsciously, influenced by the powerful paradigm of the mathematico-scientific. They have nearly all tended to move from the symbolic to the literal, from the personal to the impersonal, from the subjective to the objective, from the imaginative to the mathematical or empirical. The arts, I want to suggest, have without realizing it, deserted their own dimension of non-discursive expressive symbolism and entered a dimension where the methods of work and the holding categories are essentially alien. This has resulted, over all, in a symbolic impoverishment of our environment, unparalleled in any other civilization.

It is not a question of attacking the mathematico-scientific mode of investigation or order of knowledge. Within its own dimension, it is a great achievement: a noble expression of the mind seeking meaning about logic and about the nature of matter. *The tragedy has been that this mode of knowing has been elevated above all others and has been established in Western societies as the exclusive means for understanding all types of phenomena.* It has culminated in an intellectual totalitarianism such that every other category of knowing – the ethical, the aesthetic, the existential – longed to cluster inside its walls and so come to possess both its seeming infallibility and its unquestioned social status. It was in this movement, at work in the humanities for the last 100 years but perhaps in the arts only strongly present during the last thirty years, that the damage was done. Qualities previously associated with the artist's mission – inwardness, passion, vision, personality, intensity of experience – under the mathematico-scientific paradigm came to be regarded as 'outdated', and more public and more impersonal qualities were thought to be essential. The visual arts thus began to seek their meaning and justification through adopting the concepts and even the working-methods of science. They wanted to be allied with the industrial and technocratic process.

Some of the manifestoes made by artists during the 'sixties' show only too clearly the mesmerizing power of the mathematico-scientific category. Frank Popper in characterisitic euphoria claimed: 'Art will become an industrial product ... Art will become pure research like science'. Vasarely proclaimed that the individual artist had now been superseded: 'From now on only teams, groups or whole disciplines can create: cooperation between scientists, engineers, technicians, architects and plasticians will be the *sine qua non* of the work of art.' In 1967, in his preface for an exhibition of Objective Art, Otto Hahn offered a fuller statement about the relationship of art and science:

The more this Objective Art emerges, the more it reflects the great turning-point of twentieth-century thought: objectivity and the acceptance of artifice. What men want is not impressions but facts. Facts furnished by a system: economic, sociological, psychoanalytical, statistical, photographic ... Man in search of an authenticity in accordance with Nature and the Cosmos has given way to man finding harmony in the artificiality of the technological, industrial, mechanized world, finding pleasure and beauty in the products of synthesis and substitution ... Science today is erecting artificial means which will soon consign Nature to prehistory ...[9]

In the same preface Hahn declared with a sigh of relief:

No more brushes, no more painting, no more eye, no more hand, no more play of materials, no more feeling, no more personality.[10]

Instead we have objects; Hahn's exhibition of objective art displayed a pair of ironing boards, a gun mounted on tyres, a wardrobe, a raincoat stuck fast to a piece of formica and other such artificial pieces. What we find here is, I believe, a total confusion about the nature of art and the nature of human nature. *Art has never been primarily concerned with pure objectivity or the documenting of facts* – its first and distinguishing task has always been to give visual form to subjective experience, to the emotional, imaginative, and sensuous experience of the living subject. When art has concerned itself exclusively with documentation – as in the late Victorian period – it has invariably been a sign of declining energies and cultural ossification.

One could take each of Hahn's sentences in turn and reveal the crassness of thought they exemplify. Fortunately there is no need to do that. The whole of English letters since the time of William Blake has, with a certain monumental magnificence, revealed the total inadequacy of the mathematico-scientific paradigm to understand the inner and existential dimensions of human life. Yet it is depressing to see artists in our own time extinguishing the bright torches of their forerunners and allying themselves with the brutal technocratic thrust of material civilization. It is depressing to see Gradgrind emerge in the twentieth century not as a utilitarian teacher but as an objective artist! It testifies to the formidable power of the single mathematico-scientific paradigm and its negative shadow, its attendant taboo on inwardness, on feeling, sensuality, and expression.

I have taken a few declarations of intent by artists to show how there is a marked tendency to justify art in terms of science and technology. It could be said I have chosen my artists carefully and that they are in no way representative. Certainly there are important exceptions. I would argue that the artists I have quoted *do* represent a very characteristic tendency in the contemporary art scene and that, furthermore, this tendency can be detected by an analysis of the style of language now often used in art discourse, and in the current rhetoric of art colleges.

It is revealing that in many art colleges it has become fashionable to talk about drawing as 'a mode of inquiry' as 'visual research', and 'the assembling of data'. A similar metal-edged language can also be found in *Studio International* which advocated in one issue the need

> to recomplicate the picture surface once the initial statement of its programmatic purity had become a general reflex.[11]

The language derives from mechanistic psychology which is, of course, psychology transfixed in the mathematico-scientific paradigm. 'Reflex' and 'programmatic' are terms one would expect to find in some dull American set text on behavioural psychology. And even the word 'statements', often employed in the discussion of painting and sculpture, with its connotation of emotional neutrality and its openness to public verifiability, derives its status from the empirical procedures characteristic of scientific method. Behind such an impersonal language there lies an unconscious but nevertheless real denigration of human subjectivity, of emotional exposure and personal vision. Just to give one example of such a denigration, consider Max Kozlaff's assertion in *Studio International*.

> the non-verbalized preliminary work will elicit that final playfulness between stimuli and response which we dignify by saying that we have been moved.[12]

This is a characteristic placing of reductive theory before the actuality of experience. The being moved is the primary experience, *is the reality*, is quite irreducible; yet here we have a critic who is ready to make the cold abstractions of stimuli/response primary and to demote the experience as secondary. In all this there would seem to be at work a search for a machinery of functions rather than an openness to the immediate experiences of consciousness: a desire for mechanism and abstraction which negates that which we should possess most strongly, the complex daily plenitude of our own experience. Theory is elevated over experience and becomes crassly reductive.

Ian Stephenson described a winning picture at the John Moore's prestigious Liverpool Exhibition in the following way:

> real random response rejects
> 'compositional' certainty completely
> & dejects design determinism
> into *individible* indeterminism instead.
> an atomical appli*cation*
> utilizing ultimate units u
> *pio*neers particle painting
> (quantity = quality) *physicalyrical*.
> cf. cubofuturist configurative creationfields.
> spectacular space/particular place. [13]

What does such a language – the language of mechanical stasis – tell us about the condition of contemporary art? I am arguing that it points to a widespread, if ill-conceived, attempt to dissolve the human and binding categories of art and an attempt to recouch them in terms derived from science, mathematics, and technology. Many contemporary movements in the visual arts have aspired towards an objectivity – we recall Otto Hahn's plea 'No more personality!' – which art cannot, by its very nature, possess. This false desire for pure objectivity has resulted in an art alienated from the perennial sources of creativity and in an art whose audience is as artificial as its product, being made up not of a sympathetic diverse public but only of art-critics, art-dealers, and art-bureaucrats. It has led to an anti-art feeding off cerebral theories, forever spiralling inwards, forever out of contact with forces which might shake its self-rotating equilibrium.

Objectivity, however, is not the only misplaced category in the contemporary visual arts; so too is the category 'progress' which, once again, derives largely from the mathematico-scientific realm. In science, where one theory builds upon another, where an old theory is discarded in the light of a new theory, where with the passing of each century and even decade there would seem to be an ever greater understanding of the physical nature of the universe, it would seem right to talk, with a few qualifications, of progress. Science is cumulative, is developmental: it does advance, significantly, through time. But the fact that there is such progress in science gives us no reason to believe that it is so in other dimensions of the human mind. In art, historically, we can locate high periods of vitality and periods of stagnation, but we cannot plot a linear development in which the new constantly surpasses the old. Henry Moore is not greater than Rodin, Rodin is not greater than Michelangelo, Michelangelo is not greater than Phidias. In an important sense, the Palaeolithic cave-drawings of the bison cannot be surpassed. Indeed, in the arts we often notice not a progression but a regression, a failure to maintain the aesthetic and spiritual levels of the past. If, to take an obvious example, we look at modern public architecture and then at Gothic public architecture, we have little choice but to regard the Medieval work – the anonymous artefacts of the so-called Dark Ages before the Enlightenment – as infinitely more expressive and coherent.

The category of linear progress, so pertinent in science, does not illuminate the arts, and yet many have wished to establish it there. Here, for example, is the artist Vasarely:

> The art idea is quitting its age old fogs to luxuriate in the sunshine of the vast network of modernity which is being woven round the globe.[14]

And this, even more tellingly, is the artist Schoffer:

> Contemporary painting and sculpture don't interest me. Can you imagine anyone nowadays building a factory for the construction of horse-drawn carriages? Of course not! Well it's the same with art: brushes were all right for painting and mallets for sculpture between the fourteenth and seventeenth centuries.[15]

Naïvely, and without question, the artist assumes that there must be a parallel between technology and art: that as one progresses from the horse-drawn carriage to the motorcar, so must the other possess a comparable linear forward thrust. The past, it is assumed, can tell us nothing; all that we need is given in the present and, moreover, whatever we do it must represent 'progress', be the aesthetic extension and fulfilment of all that has gone before. The power of such an assumption can be registered if we consider the unconditional praise which is locked in the word 'progressive' when applied to the arts, and the unmitigated opprobrium connected with the word 'reactionary' to define a person who has the blindness to oppose the latest expression of the artistic *avant-garde*.

It would require a volume to show how the concept of progress has affected the arts. Within a restricted context, the word can, of course, be meaningfully applied: an artist does progress in his work, a movement can also be seen to develop and become more complex in the course of time ... But applied indiscriminately, the notion of inevitable progress can culminate in an appalling shallowness of mind which yet has the audacity to regard itself as the ultimate development in cultural matters. It can encourage a profound ignorance of the past, locking man into the narrow provincialism of the merely contemporary. It can make us defenceless before the tyranny of fashion and the whim of the instant moment. It can result in art colleges where the traditional techniques of drawing are not transmitted and where students can leave with little more than an ability to make a line across a map, play kinetic tricks with black and white paint, and chant pseudo-revolutionary platitudes. For these reasons it is well to be aware that there is no unambiguous linear development in the arts. One movement cannot be collapsed into another and given an evolutionary explanation. Art can regress as well as progress. It can also stagnate. Furthermore, the value of art is not in some abstract development historically conceived, but in the unique individual works of artists which, as we respond to them in all their specificity, impart their vision.

I have argued that inevitable progress and pure objectivity are misplaced categories in art discourse. There is one further related misconception, which again I think derives from the scientific and technological domain. There is a prevailing notion that any object or event can be constituted a work of art. Otto Hahn, the proponent of objective art already mentioned, celebrates 'a literal, factual art', 'a physical art' in which 'the illusion of the event is replaced by the event itself'. But art cannot be literal, cannot dispense with the illusion, and remain art. Art involves artifice, the making of an artefact which mediates and symbolizes consciousness. Art, we can say, is not life but the mediation of life through the form-seeking energies of the creative mind. Deny the symbol, deny the illusion, and we have denied art. It is because of the principle of symbolism that we can seriously ask whether, for example, a steel slab or a group of bricks or some folded blankets or two ironing boards can form works of art. Defending Robert Morris's *Slab* in the Tate Gallery, Michael Compton in his introduction to the Arts Council brochure *Art as Thought Process* wrote:

> At a certain level of consideration there is absolutely no amibiguity about such a sculpture as SLAB by Robert Morris. No matter how you look at it it remains clear that it is just what was intended and at first glance just what you see.[16]

A slab is a slab is a slab. But the real question is whether a slab can form a work of art; that is, whether it can symbolize, in any meaningful sense, some portion of compelling human experience. I think the answer has to be in the negative and that the slabs, bricks, bottles, nappies, ironing boards, and other detritus raised without visual

Plate 15   Robert Morris, *Untitled, 1966*.
Art is revelation, not representation. 'Works' like the one reproduced here are merely symptomatic of a literalism of mind which is virtually incapable of any kind of expressive symbolization.

comparison or commentary lie on the other side of what constitutes true art. They are not, like the Dadaist antics, anti-art: they are non-art. For true art to exist we must convert the mindless stasis of 'it is what it is' to the mindful transformation of 'it is what it symbolizes'. Art is revelation, not representation. The fallacy of literalism, like the fallacy of objectivity and progress, derives from a society which can accord significance only to fact and figure, to testable unambiguous data and hard statistics; in brief, to the working methods and principles of science.

Conclusion

The German philosopher Heidegger in his book *Discourse on Thinking* warned that:

The approaching tide of technological revolution in the atomic age could so captivate, bewitch, dazzle and beguile man that calculative thinking may some day come to be accepted and practiced *as the only* way of thinking. What great danger then might move upon us? Then there might go hand in hand with the greatest ingenuity in calculative planning and inventing, indifference toward meditative thinking, total thoughtlessness. And then? Then man would have denied and thrown away his own special nature – that he is a meditative being. Therefore, the issue is the saving of a man's essential nature. Therefore, the issue is keeping meditative thinking alive.[17]

Traditionally, the great function of the arts has been to keep meditative thinking alive and agile – a thinking rooted in existence, a thinking which included within itself passion, instinct, sense perception and imagination; a deep personal intuitive thinking in and through the actual context, thrust, and resistance of the world. The first flowering of modernism in the arts conferred a great freedom to such meditative thinking. The artist, it was asserted, had to be free to explore not only his relationship to things but to his own inner world, to his dreams and phantasies, and to the archaic archetypes which were buried beneath them. He was free to create those symbols which most faithfully embodied his experience. The results of this movement were and remain momentous: in our own century the works of Picasso, of Chagall, of Henry Moore, of Nolde, of Paul Klee, of David Jones express an astonishing diversity, a vitality of spirit, and an acute awareness of the principles of art. It is only in the last thirty years that what might be crudely termed the second movement of Modernism expressed in all manner of pseudo-movements, dependent on journalism and commercialism, and founded on narrow cultish principles (such as the obsession in some schools for the flat surface) has taken the arts into an arid waste-land. In this lecture I have suggested that this second movement, unlike the first movement of Modernism, seems to have been darkly infected by wholly inappropriate concepts taken from the mathematico-scientific paradigm. Instead of keeping open the existential dimension and extending the principle of expressive form, the arts (with many important exceptions) have tended to board in the house of consciousness, becoming more and more exclusive, narrow, and specialist in their concerns. And this at the very point when mechanical civilization as never before required a corrective in the life of articulate feeling and fertile imagination. The artist in merely reflecting his civilization has come to betray it.

It seems to me that the tiny minority who care about the arts are now impatiently waiting for those artists who have the courage to embody their own vital experience of life, who have the courage in a technocratic age to remain vulnerable and human, who can again give specific form to the great complexities of our natures and in so doing provide the viewers with those powerful images in which they can find their own latent humanity, and find it deeper, stronger and greater than they suspected. The emerging criticism of the prevailing cults exists to clear the ground for such art. Although all the established energies in contemporary society would conspire against it, we must yet fight for a great outcome.

Notes

1. STRONG, R. (1980) in *The Listener*, 20 November.
2. PENNY, N. (1981) *The Sunday Times*, November.
3. FULLER, P. (1982) *Aesthetics after Modernism*, Writers & Readers, p. 1.
4. READ, H. (1968) *The Limits of Permissiveness* published in *The Black Rainbow*, Heinemann Educational Books, 1975, p. 5
5. MUMFORD, L. (1971) *The Pentagon of Power*, Secker & Warburg.
6. WOLFE, T. (1975) *The Painted Word*, Bantam Books, pp. 52-6.
7. AUTY, G. (1977) *The Art of Self Deception*, Libertarian Books, pp. 135-6.
8. AMAYA, M. (1965) *Pop as Art*, Studio Vista, p. 17.
9. HAHN, O. (1977) quoted in Helene Parmelin *Art Anti-Art*, Marion Boyars p. 21.
10. *Ibid.*
11. Quoted in AUTY, G. (1977) *op cit.,* p. 2
12. *Ibid.*
13. *Ibid.*
14. Quoted in Helene Parmelin (1977) *op cit*, p. 61.
15. *Ibid.*
16. COMPTON, M. (1974) *Art as Thought Process*, Arts Council.
17. HEIDEGGER, M (1959) *Discourse on Thinking*, Harper & Row, p. 56.

Chapter 6
Patterns to Which Growth May Aspire:
The Place of Myth in Education

What is omitted ... is the imagination and that omission strikes
me as irreversibly disastrous. Imagination is the fourth faculty
in addition to the Sense, the Understanding and Reason.
>   Goethe on reading Kant's *Critique of Pure Reason*.

In order to make up our minds we must know how we feel
about things; and to know how we feel about things we need
the public images of sentiment that only ritual, myth and art can
provide.
>   C. Geertz

Preamble

*Our world is only partly given: for the most part it is made; and it is made through
the symbol-making energies of the human mind.*

*These symbol-making energies and the symbolic formations they give birth to can
be seen to divide into different categories, each with its own particular grasp of
'reality', each with its own laws, procedures and characteristics. They have the
power to reveal (or, indeed, to distort) quite specific and quite essential aspects of
life.*

*Myth, seen as one distinct way of symbolising experience, is pre-eminently
concerned, though not necessarily consciously so, with the dramatic personification
and elaboration of our complex psyche. Myth provides a unique metaphoric
language for inward being, giving access to depths of the mind which might
otherwise be entirely inaccessible.*

These are the central propositions which I aim to establish in this
chapter. But before I can embark upon such large themes I feel obliged

in the present context of instrumental educational change to defend a broad imaginative and intellectual conception of education. This means that in the opening part of the chapter I attempt, therefore, to distinguish between true and false forms of education; I then move to the central notion of the plurality of symbolic forms, and conclude with an analysis of the meaning of myth and of its due place in the aesthetic curriculum.

In defining and celebrating the mythic and the mythological this chapter is also intended to offer a creative reply to the nullity of Late Modernism which I described in the last chapter. I want to leave the suggestion in the readers mind that in the cultivation of the mythopoeic we may find much of the energy necessary for a cultural renewal beyond Modernism. In my view, all the arts should be actively concerned with a further distinctive elaboration (for our own time) of the great archetypal images and the ancient narratives. The way back, providing we can hold on to the necessary Socratic complexity (which consciously distinguishes between divided and separate symbolic worlds) may be, paradoxically, the way forward.

Introduction

It is now impossible not to be aware of the attempt by the government, by industry and by the mass media to reduce education to schooling, and to reduce schooling to instrumental training and certification. All the leading political parties in the Western world are committed to the imperatives of economic growth and technological advance and, all but inevitably, see schools as instruments for materialist expansion. This is particularly true of the Conservative Government and its 1988 Education Reform Bill which threatens both to standardize education through central control and, at the same time, put much of its organization in the hands of impersonal and uninformed 'market forces'.

The great weakness of the instrumental view is that it deprives education of any coherent, enduring content. Because it confers to the prevailing power group, the right to determine the goals of education, it renders the subject-matter of education highly relative. Indeed, under the logic of such a concept, education becomes one aspect of social engineering, the ends being determined by the power-élites in the society whatever the morality. In many government formulations the words 'education' and 'training' virtually merge into one. And this is exactly what happens under the momentum of the instrumental drive. The inward and transcendent denotations and connotations of words are erased and in their place operational definitions slickly inserted. Education for meaning becomes reduced to training in techniques. The philosophical and aesthetic are ousted by the technical. The teacher, a civil servant with a job 'to do', is given in exchange for the loss of range and freedom the reward of a quite spurious security. Yet the very concept 'education' resists the technocratic deal for it is a word which in its normal contexts, as well as in its etymological origins, points to a positive and evolving process, a process open, broad and intrinsically valuable. If we talk about the mass-media 'educating' the young or the Third Reich 'educating' adolescents to become warders of concentration camps, the word has an ironic twist simply because of its traditional and humane reference, its inherited ethical meaning. When we refer to an educated woman, we do not describe a woman who has simply mastered the skills of a number of circumscribed processes; we refer to the range, depth and acuity of her mind, to her ability to think her own thoughts, understand her own feelings; and to her ability to connect these with the feelings and thoughts of others in her relationships and through the main symbolic forms of our inherited culture.

The word itself points us away from technicism to the authentic concerns of our being. But how can we further delineate this concept of education? And what traditions of reflection and pedagogy can we as teachers, draw on to inform our analysis of contemporary functionalism and sustain our resistance to it?

The Great Tradition of English Education

In our own literary, philosophical and pedagogic traditions, particularly in the writings and practical teaching-methods of those in the nineteenth and twentieth century literary and aesthetic tradition (in Coleridge, Arnold and Leavis, in Ruskin, William Morris and Herbert Read) we can, I think, locate many of the key elements of an alternative conception of education. For example, in *English for the English*, a seminal book not only on English but also on education published in 1920, George Sampson attacked the pernicious doctrine that elementary education was there to convert children into factory hands and made an eloquent plea for a universal concept of education (although the distorting sexism seriously limits the power of the formulation):

Once more I beg the reader not to confuse education with the acquisition of knowledge, of which a man may have much and still be uneducated. A boy goes to school not to get a final stock of information, but to learn how he may go on learning, and to learn that going on is worth while. A humane education has no material end in view. It aims at making men, not machines; it aims at giving every human creature the fullest development possible to it, Its cardinal doctrine is 'the right of every human soul to enter, unhindered except by the limitations of its own powers, and desires, into the full spiritual heritage of the race'. It aims at giving 'the philosophic temper, the gentle judgement, the interest in knowledge and beauty for their own sake' that mark the harmoniously developed man. Humanism is a matter of life, not of a living'.[1]

Elsewhere in the book, Sampson defines education as initiation: 'a progressive cooperative initiation into the uttered and embodied life of man'. This is a concise definition; it anticipates the argument for a total curriculum and for the notion of education as initiation into such a whole curriculum to which I will return later in this chapter – for it forms one of the central premises of this book.

At the same time as Sampson was writing, the emerging Progressive movement in England was likewise insisting on education for life and not for 'a living' and, in the argument, emphasized the need for emotional development. Greening Lamborn, for example, in his Preface to *The Teaching of English: a New Approach* (by Tomkinson, published in 1921) wrote:

> What Greek literature did for the few of the past, English literature must do for the many of the future. The new ideal in the elementary school is indeed the old ideal in the universities – an education not so much concerned with livelihood as with living. *What is really new is the revelation of the importance of the emotional life and of the need to cultivate and enrich it* by humanistic treatment of all our studies ... to provide that culture of the feelings without which, as John Stuart Mill discovered, all intellectual culture is in vain.[2] (my emphasis)

The reference to Mill takes us further back into the nineteenth century to two other major texts: Mill's *Autobiography* (first written between 1853 and 1856) and Dickens' *Hard Times* (1854), each, in their markedly different ways, developing a critique of utilitarian concepts of education. Mill works, of course, within the inherited tradition of Utilitarianism, and part of the autobiography is an attempt to transform that narrow school of thinking from within. 'The revelation of the importance of the emotional life' comes in Chapter 5, entitled *A Crisis in My Mental History: One Stage Onward*, where having shown how the inveterate habit of analysis eroded the necessary and complementary life of feeling and passion, Mill develops *a total concept of education*:

> I had now learnt by experience that the passive susceptibilities needed to be cultivated as well as the active capacities, and required to be nourished and enriched as well as guided. The maintenance of a due balance among the faculties now seemed to me of primary importance. The cultivation of the feelings became one of the cardinal points in my ethical and philosophical creed. And my thoughts and inclinations turned in an increasing degree towards whatever seemed capable of being instrumental to that object.[3]

Analysis of the autobiography discloses that Mill may not have achieved the psychic wholeness he was seeking but, nevertheless, *the conception* is there and so are the recorded debts to Wordsworth and Coleridge, which take us further back into the substantial English literary and pedagogic tradition I am invoking.

It is not a mere coincidence that Dickens published *Hard Times* a year after Mill had started work on his autobiography. Both books have common concerns: utilitarianism, education, the life of feeling, the place of phantasy. The breakdown of John Stuart Mill, with its source in his father's ruthless pedagogy, with its systematic denial of all emotional claims, is arrestingly close to Louisa's plight as a result of her father's Utilitarian educational system. Louisa, it will be recalled, complains that her phantasies, emotions and aspirations had never had a chance to develop, for all that she had been given were 'problems which could be solved' and 'realities which could be grasped'. 'You have trained me so well', she declares, 'that I never had a child's dream'. It's worth noting here how Louisa refers to Gradgrind's work as training, a fitting of the self into patterns already predetermined, patterns which, in the case of Louisa in fiction and Mill in life, were totally alien to the entelechy of their being. *Hard Times* is an imaginative manifesto for true education against the false education of Coketown, symbol of economic industrial growth and the technicism of mind which informs and supports it.

In Sampson (developing the work of Matthew Arnold and anticipating the Cambridge School of English), in Lamborn and Tomkinson (moving, with John Stuart Mill, out of Benthamism) and in Dickens (working in and extending the great tradition of the English novel), teachers can locate a powerful, radical concept of education: *education as the many-sided development of the individual within the culture*, as initiation into the major symbolic forms of the mind in its quest for meaning and psychic wholeness. Just as F.R. Leavis helped to document (however partially) the great tradition of the English novel, so it would be possible to draw up the great tradition of English education, a tradition which with its eloquent and positive powers of formulation (as well as its biases and lacunae) attempted to check the growing technicism of the Western European mind; a response, at once creative and critical, to the emerging technology of industrial society. It is precisely this tradition that we need now in order to resist and undermine the present movement towards the dual control of education by an instrumental government and by brute market forces.

The Symbolic Forms of Knowing and the Curriculum of the Mind

Having given grounds for understanding education as an 'ultimate category', I want now to consider the various symbolic forms of knowing which are open to humankind and which, taken together, comprise, as it were, the curriculum of the mind. This returns us to one of the main themes of Chapter 2.

Here language can be deceptive. We talk about 'knowledge' in the singular and never in the plural, as though all knowing was of the same order. In our own time we tend to assume that all knowledge is 'objective', based on some sort of common verification or quantification, and that any claims, not fitting scientific criteria, are, as we say, 'merely subjective', if not illusory. Knowledge for us has to be public and measurable. But as Louis Arnaud Reid, Ernst Cassirer and Susanne Langer have reminded us, the scientific form of 'knowing', for all its importance and its present power in society, *only represents one partial way of knowing the world*. To grant it a monopoly of interpretation (as has so frequently happened) is to obscure the diverse forms of knowing which attend and illuminate our daily experience. For if knowledge is a singular noun, we yet employ the active verb in many different ways. The way Adam knew Eve was entirely different from the way he knew the number of animals in the garden. The active verb similarly covers a variety of processes:

I *know* the answer to the maths problem;
I *know* Aunty Jane;
I *know* Michelangelo's *Pietà*;
I *know* where California is;
I *know* the meaning of 'Plutocracy'.

In each case a different form of knowing has been encased in that deceptively simple verb: deductive, relational, aesthetic, informational, semantic. The consciousness of man meets its divers experience through diverse symbolic forms, each building up its own language, its own disposition, possibilities, procedures, each slowly becoming differentiated from the others.

Socrates distinguished between the ethical, the mythical and the scientific, and chose for his own extraordinary life's work the cultivation of the ethical; his teaching was developed to disturb individuals into ethical awareness. Cardinal Newman in his *Idea for a University* – another vital text in the tradition of English education – saw the critical importance of bringing the various disciplines together because, he claimed, 'they complete, correct, balance each other'. The need was to comprehend the disciplines in their totality, to see the architecture of the curriculum as a whole.

Each symbolic form represents one type of manifestation of the constructive energy of the human mind. Each symbolic form represents a different way of giving order and shape to our multitudinous experience. As I have indicated, no form can possess a monopoly in explanation, in truth. The power and efficacy of each symbolic form depends upon the context in which it is being employed. How could mathematics, in its pure form, elucidate mythology? How could chemistry, in its pure form, interpret the human complexities of history? We do not live in one world. We live in many. As organisms we live in the natural order, but through our consciousness we inhabit also a symbolic universe, a universe of the mind. of meanings, of values, of dilemmas and decisions. We live in an outer world of political and social events, as members of society; but we also drift through an inner world of spontaneous phantasy, mood and half-conscious monologue. At many points in our lives we struggle to think rationally about issues, weighing up judiciously the pros and cons of a particular problem, but at night, in sleep, we open ourselves, willingly or unwillingly, to the irrational, to dream images, with their strange purposes and elusive meanings. To reduce the tangled complexity of our experience to any one category and to make everything explainable in terms of it is not to meet the true challenge of our consciousness but rather to evade it. Such solutions lead to dissolutions. And the mind instead of remaining open to itself becomes possessed by ideology. In the nineteenth century Marx took the category of the economic and placed it at the base of human life. Upon this base everything in life was constructed. In terms of this base every manifestation of life could be properly comprehended. *One principle* acted as the key by which everything else could be unlocked. At about the same time, Compte asserted that the foundation was to be discovered in mechanics. The laws of mechanics could explain the edifice of human life. Society and history could be understood in terms of forces, pressures, the blind workings of matter in motion. The methods of the natural sciences could be used, he claimed, substantially unchanged, by social and cultural studies. In the twentieth century Freud made the single foundation the id, the cauldron of wild instincts, which had to be suppressed and so gave birth to the super-ego and the ego. Once again, the concept provided a single unifying principle by which all manifestations of life could be understood, explained. Each testifies to the *mania for one principle* which runs through Western civilization like a destructive plague. In Chapter 5 I tried to indicate how the visual arts have been severely impoverished by taking their sense of meaning from the dominant mathematico-scientific paradigm. And throughout the book I have indicated the dangers of allowing the one principle of market forces to determine all aspects of civilization. Against the temptation to assert one principle, one absolute cause for understanding of all the manifestations of individual and social life, we need to be more generous and to assert *a plurality of principles* and the possibility that we live simultaneously in a number of dimensions. We struggle to live where all the lines intersect. There would seem to be *no* single explanatory system. Man, wrote Thomas Browne in *Religio Medici*, is 'that great and true Amphibian whose nature is disposed to live, not only like other creatures in diverse elements, but in divided and distinguished worlds'.

Our task is to create through education a society which provides the best conditions for all the diverse symbolic forms of the psyche, the best conditions for exploring all the divided and distinguished worlds which comprise our human world. How to develop the mind which can think rationally and yet is also responsive to the eloquence of myth; which is ready to appreciate the efficacy of scientific methods and yet is open to the illumination of the arts; a psyche that can think well, sense well, feel well and dream well? We need a curriculum based on a plurality of principles, in which the diverse symbolic forms are energetically represented and their various truths given proper space and deference. This is not the place to present, in detail, what could be called a total curriculum, or to delineate, with due qualification, the symbolic forms which might comprise it. I have suggested an outline for such a curriculum in Chapter 2. Here I am concerned to understand the mythic mode of formulation. I have mentioned the eloquence of myth, but to understand myth we must go much deeper, we have to take our pick-axes to the frozen surface of received thought and current linguistic use. In fact, we must reach to the other side of an extraordinary life-negating prejudice against the mythic, which in a technical civilization confronts us on most sides. We will have to come at the problem at different angles, using different implements, if we are to get below the current incomprehension in this great matter.

The Misinterpretation of the Mythic Mode

It is significant that even the words myth/mythic/mythical are thoroughly problematic because by common usage they refer not to a particular mode of symbolic formulation but to a form of falsehood, inaccuracy or deception. Something 'mythical' is something erroneous. This in itself is revealing for such uses in language faithfully record a civilization's underlying assumptions; but, perhaps, even more revealing is the fact that this particular use of the word 'mythical' dates from the latter part of the nineteenth century, the age of Positivism and of the natural sciences. According to the poet Kathleen Raine: 'the art of a secular society has suffered fatally from the identification of knowledge with natural science'. Certainly it would seem likely that the identification of all knowledge with the specific knowledge open to the natural sciences has led to the use of 'myth' to denote falsehood. Instead of myth being comprehended as a distinct symbolic form, metaphorical rather than literal in nature, it was interpreted as a rudimentary science which, in nearly every case, could be judged quite unambiguously as being false. Thus the word 'myth' became not only synonymous with false, but also frequently carried such connotations as being outmoded, superstitious and simplistic. The expression 'It's a pure myth, that' embodies a deep and fatal confusion of symbolic categories.

The habit of interpreting myth according to other categories is, though, centuries old. The Greeks themselves, in the twilight of their civilization, looked back on their myths in an attempt to make intellectual sense of them. They developed three different, though sometimes connected, interpretations. Firstly, it was argued that the gods were historical figures deified by their societies and turned into legends. Secondly, it was suggested that the myths were philosophical and moral allegories – they could be transposed into abstract terms and in this manner, comprehended; they constituted an early form of moral philosophy and with the right keys their meanings could be opened and understood. Thirdly, it was argued, the myths charted the distant stars and planets. The mythical figures of the stars were expelled into outer space but their great distance from human life did not prevent their influencing human action and temperament. All the constellations were given mythological significance and the signs of the Zodiac connected with mythical heroes. Mythology, under this approach, became a curious fusion of science and astrology. In his closely documented *The Survival of the Pagan Gods*, Jean Seznec demonstrates how these three streams of mythological interpretation ran into the medieval world, forming curious confluences with the dominant myth, Christianity. The Renaissance according to Seznec did not 'discover' the Pagan gods, as is commonly alleged, but continued to draw on medieval traditions, sources and texts only *in a style* that became more and more recognizably 'classical'. They brought the light of reason and a more comprehensive sense of human existence to bear on the mythological figures; but somehow, that very light distorted, in some degree, the nature of the mythopoeic; for, as we shall see, the mythopoeic image possesses a spontaneity and compelling energy often lacking in the great formal canvasses of the Renaissance painters. Yet the renaissance did represent a high-point in mythic image-making, depicting a multifarious process of Christian saints and Pagan gods, of Christ and Pan, of the Blessed Virgin Mother and Aphrodite, of Saint Peter and sage Plato. And, certainly, from the Renaissance down to our own times, through the iconoclastic Reformation, through the Enlightenment to the technicism of modern society, we witness, with all manner of minor and major resistances, a continuous denial and suppression of the deep mythic and image-making impulse. Any adequate analysis would here have to demonstrate the unconscious fear of the image revealed in the barbaric destruction of statues, carvings and tapestries which occurred on a large scale during the Reformation; it would have to consider the immeasurable disdain that the key figures of the Enlightenment felt for all that was primitive, medieval, archaic and mythical in form. It would have to evaluate the increasingly abstract and mechanical notion of life disseminated by the Promethean development of the sciences; it would have to document also the corresponding symbolic narrowing of Christianity, finally leaving the isolated individual soul with his own private leap of faith into the absurd God, without ikon, ritual or communal ceremony. And, finally, such an analysis would have to consider the effects of industrial society on communal symbol-making. As we will see in the next chapter, such an analysis could find relevant material in the empty formalism and stark minimalism of contemporary art. It could find further material in the flat surfaces and clinical lines of modern architecture, in the sterilised environments of our offices and factories, even in the lifeless boxes of our educational institutions, in the classrooms, lecture theatres and seminar rooms of abstract knowledge and mental calculation. Most of our drab technical environment negates the deep need of the psyche for true images of being, though advertising surrounds us with its bastardized mythology, with the gods and goddesses daily rising out of soap, toothpaste, cars, bras and consumer trivia.

Yet like Orpheus, whose floating head continued to sing even after his body had been savaged by the Maenads, a myth may be dismembered or abused but it does not seem to die. Philosophers who denied the mythopeic were yet compelled to sustain it. Karl Marx, in the name of reason, established in his scientific work a mythological battleground in which good and evil raged until a final Garden of Eden had been achieved, the state withered and man came into his own kingdom perpetually. It was the questionable achievement of Marx to give the archetype of Paradise a future tense. Freud, trying to clinically document the dark forces of the psyche, could not advance without raising the mythical figures of Oedipus and Electra, Thanatos and Eros (seen as warring opposites), and even his typology of id, ego and super-ego, in a pale and abstract manner, mythical in quality. It is surely true also that even in our technocratic society, the gods and goddesses move, in a whole variety of disguises, through our dreams, fantasies, sexual obsessions and intimate pathologies. At another level, often hopelessly trivialized, they are resurrected in comics, magazines, newspapers and, particularly, in advertising, where a whole range of heroic and dream-like figures hold out the possibility of transformation if only one buys the mythologised goods of the consumer-society. In many pop-stars one detects debased versions of Dionysus. The suppressed images return at every point – in the counterfeit mythology of the consumer society, in disturbing nightmares and eluding dreams. Indeed, at the very heart of the technocratic society lives one, heroic, masculine, compulsive

Plate 16 Redon The Floating Head of Orpheus *after 1903.*
Like Orpheus, whose head continued to sing even after his body had been savaged by the Maenads, a myth may be dismembered or abused but it does not seem to die.

god, unmodified and uncontrolled, the god of progress, now, perhaps nearing the end of his long, tyrannical phase of power.

Understanding Myth From Within its Form

It would, however, be misleading to leave the impression that the meaning of myth has been, since the time of the Renaissance, totally neglected because a handful of philosophers have, in fact, turned a sympathetic mind to analyze its nature and purposes. Giambatista Vico was one of the first. A contemporary of Descartes, Vico protested at the narrowness of the new rational philosophy and worked in his *Scienza Nuova* (first published in 1725) towards a form of philosophy which would comprehend man in his totality through a sympathetic study of all the things that he had fabricated out of his own nature: language, cities, sciences, arts, coins, laws, governments, and so forth. It was through the systematic study of these forms made by man during distinct phases of times in equally distinct cultures, that the philosopher could best come to an understanding of human nature. The study of deductive logic alone could not reveal the essential truths of existence. For Vico, mythology was one of the first symbolic forms created by humankind to make order of his world; it was a form which had faded wherever the power of reason had developed and now was almost impossible for us, to fully experience:

> But the nature of our civilized minds is so detached from the senses, even in the vulgar, by abstractions corresponding to all the abstract terms our languages abound in, and so refined by the act of writing, and, as it were, spiritualised by the use of numbers, because even the vulgar know how to count and reckon, that it is naturally beyond our power to form the vast image of this mistress called 'sympathetic nature' ... It is equally beyond our power to enter into the vast imagination of those first men, whose minds were not in the least abstract, refined or spiritualised, because they were entirely immersed in the senses, buffeted by the passions, buried in the body. That is why we said above that we can scarcely understand, still less imagine, how those first men thought who forwarded gentile humanity.[4]

In Vico the rationalizations of mythology – mythology as gentle allegory – fall away. The first man and woman actually experienced all phenomena as living divinities and transferred to these divinities the qualities of their own bodies. Through metaphor man made of himself an entire universe. It is noteworthy Vico remarks:

> that in all languages the greater part of the expressions relating to inanimate things are formed by metaphor for the human body and its parts and from the human senses and passions.[5]

Thus, in our own language, for example, we talk of the mouth of a river or cave or opening, the shoulders of a hill, the lip of a cup, the veins of a rock, the heart of a storm, the bowels of the earth, the foot of the mountain. These metaphors derive from our own body, but once they were as the physical elements of all the gods present in an animate universe; a mythopoeic universe. In Vico, there is the recognition of the imaginative and sensuous power of myth, and the realization that while it was experienced by primitive man as simply true, it is, in fact, metaphorical in form, telling us more about the nature of human nature than the nature of the physical universe. He claimed:

For when we wish to give utterance to our understanding of spiritual things, we must seek aid from our imagination to explain them and, like painters, form human images of them. But these ideological poets, unable to make use of the understanding, did the opposite and more sublime thing: they attributed senses and passions ... to bodies, and to bodies as vast as sky, sea and earth. Later, as these vast imaginations shrank and the power of abstraction grew,[1] the personifications were reduced to diminutive signs.[6]

The Greek theories which I listed earlier can be understood as a continuation of this movement from multifaceted metaphor to referential meaning, from rich unconscious personification to linear rational explanation.

Schelling, the German Romantic philosopher, like Vico, also discards the theory of allegory and in his philosophy seeks to establish not the psychological genesis but the philosophical meaning of myth. As in Kant's philosophy, ethics and knowledge are seen to derive from the categories of the human mind, so in Schelling, myth becomes an independent form, a form which can only be properly comprehended by reference to its own informing principles. The task of the philosopher is to make explicit these principles, which unify the diverse expressions of the mythical mind. Although Schelling's work – work which was to greatly influence Coleridge – is clouded in the appalling abstractions of German Metaphysical Idealism and distorted by its cosmic absolutes, it yet points to a profound and liberating principle· that *myth is basic to the human mind, that it is an autonomous configuration of the psyche, and that it has its own laws, its own reasons, its own procedures.* It is not, in essence, elementary science, nor is it history; it, therefore, cannot be invalidated by the methods of science (a different symbolic configuration) or history (another symbolic form). Myth can be only truly apprehended from within, through its own categories and not through the alien categories of discursive forms of knowledge.

Schelling's insight is further amplified, refined and given a broader context in the work of Ernst Cassirer. In his philosophy of symbolic forms, Cassirer sees the symbol as the active and constitutive agent in the making of human experience. We bring to the world 'out there' our own symbol-making powers and so recreate it as a distinctly human universe. But the symbols we bring are not all of the same kind; each simultaneously reveals and obscures. Only by differentiating and sympathetically standing within the various symbolic forms can we have some grasp of the total world open to us. For Cassirer, as for Vico and Schelling, myth is one of these forms, the one from which all the others, with great difficulty and formidable struggle, have slowly emerged to assert their different natures: science, mathematics, the humanities, the arts. ... In the beginning was the monopoly of myth. Yet, as it was argued earlier, it is the mind's deft holding of diverse symbolic nets – each giving access to different realms of experience – that an ever-precarious balance is achieved.

Some Examples of the Mythic Mode

We have seen how the Greeks in the last phase of their great civilization understood the myths in one of three ways; as early scientific accounts of the universe, as an inflated record of historical events and figures or as philosophical and moral allegory. And, indeed, all of these interpretations, which ran through the Medieval period into the Renaissance and beyond, carry some truth – but, as has been indicated, they tend to miss the intrinsic nature of myth, the primitive impulse of myth, its tumultuous energy, its primordial beauty, its creative necessity. On the one hand the interpretations strike us as too rational, intellectual glossings on material which is far from rational; on the other hand, they seem like exercises in castration. Treated in this manner, the unmanageable and often immoral gods could be domesticated and brought as serving eunuchs into the committee meetings of high civilization. But in this way, at least the gods were kept alive in the human memory, even if their electric energy had been discharged.

How, then, are we to understand myth? The scientific, allegorical and historical interpretations are not to be totally dismissed; indeed, in spite of all we have said against them, they can be seen to have some veracity, but they do not take us to the essence of mythic consciousness. What, then, is a more comprehensive way of seeing myth? And why should it be important in contemporary education?

To begin to answer these questions let us first consider two samples of mythopoeic utterance, not in our own tradition. The following is a North American Indian song translated into English and published in the anthology *Technicians of the Sacred*:

THE BROKEN VASE
Beautiful princess
your brother
has broken

your vase,
and that is why
it thunders, why lightning flashes
and thunderbolts roll.
But you, princess
mistress of the rain
you will give us water
and, at other times
your hand will scatter hail,
or snow.
Pachacamac,
Creator of the World,
and our god Viracocha
have given you a soul
and a body
for this sole purpose[7]
    (Quechua)

The second utterance is from a statement made by Smohalla, a Nez Perce Indian, published in the same anthology:

My young men shall never work. Men who work cannot dream, and wisdom comes in dreams.

You ask me to plow the ground. Shall I take a knife and tear my mother's breast? Then when I die she will not take me to her bosom to rest.

You ask me to dig for stone. Shall I dig under her skin for bones? Then when I die I cannot enter her body to be born again.

You ask me to cut grass and make hay and sell it and be rich like white men. But how dare I cut off my mother's hair?

It is a bad law, and my people cannot obey it. I want my people to stay with me here. All the dead men will come to life again. We must wait here in the house of our fathers and be ready to meet them in the body of our mother.[8]
    (statement by Smohalla, Pez Perce Indian)

To take two fragments in translation and out of their cultural context is, I am aware, open to abuse. But I am anxious in the first place not to interpret these pieces so much as to appreciate *their mode of formulation*, not to point to their content so much as the specific manner in which the mythic impulse is given expression. If we consider the first song we can discern that it works through a naive and compelling form of personification (the elements seen as expressions of world divinities). The action is direct and quintessentially dramatic. The style is sublime and simple. The song, furthermore, evokes an incident which is placed inside a totality. What is recorded is so and not otherwise. In all of these qualities: its power of personification, its power of drama, its power of scale, its simplicity in style and its recording of a grand necessity, the cosmic order (it is thus and not otherwise), it provides a model example of mythic formulation.

The same qualities can be seen also in the second passage. The personification is, of course, not experienced as a literary device, but as a profound truth which the White Man has violated:

> You ask me to plow the ground.
> Shall I take a knife and tear my mother's breast?
> Then when I die she will not take me to her bosom to rest.[9]

Here the earth has *become* the archetypal Mother-Goddess figure found in all cultures. It provides a major clue, also, to our understanding of myth as metaphor and as the projection of metaphor across the face of the earth. In other words the metaphor is not seen as, in some way, man-made but is *experienced, as is the case with all projection, as coming from the object out there*. Ernst Cassirer analyzing this strange and deeply human process writes: 'thing and signification are undifferentiated; they concresce in an immediate unity'. It is, perhaps, no accident that the Latin 'numen' divinity sounds the same as 'nomen' (a name) or that for Christians 'the Word was with God and *the Word was God* and the Word was made Flesh'. Object and symbol fuse into what is experienced as an indivisible unity. Carl Jung, examining the process psychologically, has written that 'the projection of symbolic images is so fundamental that we have taken several thousand years of civilization to detach it in some measure from its outer object'. But in as much as we detach the symbolic image from its object, in as much as we can take it back into its source, we can begin to appreciate the origins of the mythic impulse and learn our own natures as if for the first time. In myth we discover an unexpected and powerful language for the reading of what is held within. Myth, seen in this light, is a massive and virtually unused educative energy.

Myths as Imaginal Structures in Polar Equilibrium

Put in psychological terms, the challenge is to take back into ourselves the primitive projection of sublime and daemonic images or, rather, to let the great mythical dramas work upon us in a new way.

In Greek mythology each god represents some portion of our own humanity: Prometheus represents our heroic desire to serve a great cause: Pan represents our promiscuous imaginings: Eros our desire for a fuller love; Hephaistos our will to make and create: Hermes our powers of cunning and deception. They provide us with dramatic images of elements within our own nature and in the nature of others. 'In the mythologically-instructed community', writes Jerome Bruner, a corpus of images and models are given 'that provides a pattern to which growth may aspire'. And not only images, but also dramatic narratives which embody an extraordinary balance and life-wisdom. Invariably the dramatic action carries, not in the manner of a parable but as an intrinsic part of its own movement, an equal measure of positive and negative elements. Pandora, out of insatiable curiosity, opens the box which brings so much misery and yet, at the end, the same destructive act brings the eternal consolation of hope. (Eve, in the comparable Christian myth, eats the apple which ends innocence but it remains, nevertheless, an apple from the tree of god-like knowledge). In the Icarus and Daedalus myth, the exuberant vertical flight of the boy into the sun is counterbalanced by the steady horizontal flights of the middle-aged man. The god Pan, god of instinct and sexuality, of rape, masturbation and nightmare, is complemented and completed by the elusive nymphs he endlessly pursues. As James Hillman in his excellent analysis of the Pan archetype says, 'if the nymphs and Pan are one, then no prohibition is necessary. *An inhibition is already present in the compulsion itself* ... In Pan instinct is always in search of soul' Christ, the God-man reduced to a criminal, dies on the cross between two thieves: one repents, the other refuses. Opposites define each other, complement each other. Both are necessary; without them we would have no way of identifying the complex elements of individual and social life. Myths are tensely balanced systems, imaginal structures in polar equilibrium.

Myths embody in the most lyrical and dramatic manner the abiding patterns of existence, clusters of complementary figures, an endless dialectic. The narratives poetically embody a balance between opposites and the divine characters seen together complement, correct, and fulfil each other. In the mythical totality something like a completeness of vision can be rendered; myth can give us living images of our own impulses and our own otherwise indeterminate possibilities.

In myths, our confused impulses and instincts are converted into resonant images and holding narratives. To open ourselves to their power is to open ourselves to the unconsciously projected life-wisdom of the human race. Mythical images are pedagogic images of the highest order. But they are not necessarily closed. We can adapt the myths to our own changed needs; we can change the narratives, give them a further twist. And, where there are gaps, we can create new myths. To do this is to find form for our feelings and our relationships – and to find mythic form is to develop those very feelings and to give them further meaning, an enduring significance.

The Place of Myth in the Classroom

We return to education and the curriculum. It is important that children know their fairy tales not at the high plateau of meaning we have been struggling across, but simply *as stories*, for their symbols transmit their meanings at levels below consciousness and in the language that is closest to that used by the child himself. It is also important that adolescents have an easy knowledge of the Greek and Christian myths and working knowledge of other mythological traditions; not knowing *about*, but loving knowledge *of*. At the moment there is reason to believe that this specific initiation into the vital and embodied life of man is being neglected and that, as was claimed earlier, it is being neglected because we have ceased to understand the true nature of mythical exploration and utterance.

There is one further and related task; that is the need to release in children their own myth-making impulses. They need to experience myth from within their own imagination. And it is for this reason that the teaching of the myths should enter the curriculum through the medium of the arts. It is important to stress, at this point, that the work is done intuitively and not rationally, that the symbols of mythology are not explained *but perceptually experienced*. Creative activity has to go on at a deeper level of mind than is usually engaged in our institutions of abstract learning. Seonaid Robertson, who has had a lifetime's experience of working imaginatively with mythic materials has written:

> Myths and symbols ... have their own intrinsic effect. They, of their own nature and power will plumb the human depths and

evoke change even if that never comes to the conscious mind. Some psychiatrists find it difficult to believe this but their work is in a different field and I am utterly convinced, through years of seeing the results, that the making of a symbolic object can have a most profound effect without the maker being aware of the significance of what he has made. This means that children, uneducated adults and even mental defectives can have this release without the intellectual effort of analysis and the possible concern at understanding what they have portrayed so openly. [10]

In her *Rosegarden and Labyrinth*, Seonaid Robertson gives many eloquent and moving examples of the mythical impulse at work in adolescents, as blindfolded, they shape, in relationship to immediate sensuous impulses and psychic imagery, large lumps of kneaded clay. The imaginative experience can be taken down into the inherited mythical narratives and charged by the encounter. Consider, for example, the following two pieces of writing both working within the powerful archetypal constellation of the crucifixion; the first is by a fifth-year girl, the second by a sixth former:

Crucifixion

'Paul's a dirty rotten creep!'
'Paul's a dirty rotten creep!'
Their childish, mocking voices sang with a shrill cruelty, and a heavy, choking lump blocked his throat so that he couldn't swallow.

A quick foot jerked forward and neatly kicked his shins. The blow was sharp, and painful.

Someone else banged heavily against him. His foot slipped and he lost his balance. The world span round, and the voices behind him suddenly became scared.

Someone shouted, 'He's falling off the edge!' but it was too late and each of the boys turned with a sick feeling beating in his stomach and ran crazily away.

Paul fell, and his arms went wild, waving and clutching at nothing as it swished past his ears. Then his finger-nails ripped on something cold and hard, and his finger clawed and scrabbled desperately at the solidity. The solidity crumbled, and screams twisted and distorted his face as, for a few seconds, he fought like a lunatic against gravity. Then, as the solidity became dust, his writhing body suddenly became still, and dropped like a stone onto the rocks below, where the sea washed the blood from wounds in his hands and side, forming streaks, which crossed in the water, like a crucifix. [11] (fifth-year girl)

The second passage does not take a 'profane' incident down into a 'sacred' event to leave it suggestively there; rather it directly encounters the myth of the crucifixion and moves, stumblingly, towards some recognition of the paradox of life within death:

The Brown Tree touched with Green
I stood among many, looking
At the three brown crosses
On the green hill.
I laughed and joked with
My companion, not realising
That today I would see
Myself die.
We watched the figure, motionless
And the hands ripped red
By the nails that had
Driven home their mark.
The head hung loosely on
The reddened neck.
And the proud Asian hair
Matted like straw.
And still we laughed −
The figure cried for water − but
We did not hear his
Pleas.
It was then that I really
Looked at him for the
First time,
His eyes met mine
And held them − fixed −
Among the torture of his
hanging body.
His eyes were at peace.
It was almost as though
Through the sickness of
Waiting death − he could see the
Green hills touched with
Mist

And the Spring leaves just
Beginning to burst into greenness.
It was as though he
Saw the children playing on the
Street where he had played
And that he laughed
With them as they laughed.
I could not bear those eyes
Any longer, I tore myself away
And ran panic-stricken down
the Green Hill.
Suddenly I faltered, the
Earth closed upon itself.
And there was a darkness
I have never known before —
And yet towards the east
There was a faint trace
Of Gold on the green hills.
It was then I knew there
was hope
My eyes searched for His
Eyes, frightened that I
Would find them dead,
And yet they were alive
And in the moment when
His comforting eyes met mine,
I knew through the
Strangled mystery of his body,
On the green, green, tree that
He offered me Life and Hope.[12] (F.J. Colman)

I quote the passages as examples of the kind of writing which can emerge from handling myth directly in the classroom. It is hoped that as imaginative works they speak for themselves and require no further exegesis.

The deep mythic impulse in us is intimately related to the creative impulse of the art-maker. The desire is a common one for metaphor. Herbert Read wrote:

The self, the artist is now telling us, has little or nothing to do with the conventional mask I present to the world; it can be adequately represented only by signs or symbols which have a formal equivalent to an inner world of feeling *most of which is submerged below the level of consciousness.*[13]

Read's definition of the symbol in art, though perhaps, not widely understood by contemporary artists, corresponds to our own understanding of symbol in myth. In the teaching of the aesthetic disciplines we present myths in such a way that they stand a chance of becoming part of the imaginative life of the child; we also give the child permission to become, in his or her own modest way, and through the expressive media of all the arts, a myth-maker. In this way, through mythic recreation, *the child's imagination may be developed and the symbolic culture renewed.*

Notes

1. SAMPSON, G. (1970) *English for the English*, Cambridge University Press, first printed 1921, p. 20.
2. Greening Lamborn in preface to TOMKINSON (1921) *The Teaching of English: A New Approach*, Oxford University Press.
3. MILL, J.S. *Autobiography* (first published 1873).
4. VICO, G. (1725) *The New Science*, edited by BERGIN, T. and FISCH, M. (1970) Cornell University Press, p. 76.
5. *Ibid.*
6. *Ibid.*
7. ROTHENBERG, J. (Ed) (1968) *Technicians of the Sacred*, (America.)
8. *Ibid.*
9. *Ibid.*
10. ROBERTSON, S. (n.d.) *Myth and Symbol in Education* 'Tract 29/30', Gryphon Press.
11. Quoted in ABBS, P. (1969) *English for Diversity*, Heinemann Educational Books, p. 128.
12. Unpublished writing by a sixth former from Withywood Comprehensive School, Bristol.
13. READ, H. (1955) *Icon and Idea*, Faber & Faber, p. 117.

Chapter 7
Education, Phantasy and the Inner Life of Feeling

The intensity of my feelings drove my language into metaphor. It was very exciting because the metaphors just took over and I found myself in a different plane of consciousness.

Jacqueline Langlois

We cannot take a step in life or literature without using an image. It is hard to take more than a step without narrating. Before we sleep each night we tell over to ourselves what we may also have told to others, the story of the past day. We mingle truths and falsehoods, not always quite knowing where one blends into the other. As we sleep we dream dreams from which we wake to remember, half-remember and almost remember, in forms that may be dislocated, dilapidated or deviant but are recognizably narrative.

Humankind cannot bear very much abstraction or discursive reasoning. The stories of our days and the stories in our days are joined in that autobiography we are all engaged in making and remaking, as long as we live, which we never complete, though we all know how it is going to end.

Barbarba Hardy

Preamble

In the present climate one all but shies away from presenting intimate details of one's own teaching or from using such language as 'inner life', 'the symbolic life', 'the life of feeling'. And yet, again and again, one has no choice but to acknowledge that, ultimately, it is only this kind of language which can begin to formally capture the actual essence of one's teaching and those moments of collaborative learning in the classroom, workshop and seminar.

In this chapter I argue the educational case for including in our aesthetic programme work on imagery and, in particular, that inner and continuous sequencing of imagery we call phantasy. I have no doubt that many phantasies can be self-destructive, distorting and dangerous. Many images in our society, informed by the counterfeit culture of advertising and mass-produced narratives, can offer little more than escape phantasies. However, in this chapter I am concerned to make a more positive argument. I want to suggest that at least *some* phantasies can educate, that they can contain in imaginal and perceptual form truths necessary for the development of the individual, particularly where the phantasy can be brought into productive relationship with elements in our collectively inherited mythology, religion and art.

The power of the imaginal to *re*present and *re*cognize has still to be accepted in the practice and study of education. At the moment we allow our nursery schools and primary schools to develop the life of images and narratives (although, under the instrumental pressures of our time even this is liable to disappear) but at secondary school we firmly insist that metaphors, like toys once needed but now outgrown, must be packed away and that all understanding from henceforth, will be conceptual, abstract and preferably related to 'useful knowledge'. It is an irony that fits our times perfectly that the school should be made *the agent of such an impoverishment of human thinking*, as if Shakespeare and Homer, as if Henry Moore and Rembrandt, as if Michael Tippett and Mozart, were not, in their perceptual and imaginal fields, *thinkers* of the highest order.

The chapter begins with a general diagnosis of the neglect of imagery and then presents an argument for the imaginal realm through the consideration of four diverse examples which are chosen to demonstrate its educational and cultural significance. While the argument does not directly employ the concepts of the vertical and horizontal axes of creativity developed in the opening chapter, the reader will observe that both of these notions are present in the structuring of the thought and the interpretation of the phenomenon of phantasy.

Introduction

I believe that in Western civilization we have valued concept at the expense of image and that this has culminated in an extraordinary alienation of humankind from the sources of being. Inasmuch as our schools, colleges, and universities engender only an abstract and quantitive mode of understanding, the memorizing of inert knowledge crudely measured through a plethora of mechanical examinations, they are responsible for passing on some of the darkest pathologies in Western civilization. In this chapter my intention is to restore the power of the living image, to confer on it a high epistemological status, to put it alongside concept as one of the key ways in which we symbolize and thus come to know our human world.

'No more great dreamers; no more great dreams ... Is it really such a great dream to parcel up a building or a mountain?'[1] So the painter Josef Herman has remarked in response to the nullity of much Late Modernist art. The emphasis on the word 'dream' is, I think, significant, because dreams are made up of the spontaneous imagery of the unconscious mind, imagery unmediated by intellect, imagery that, in Jungian language, we might say constitutes the symbolic equivalent of emotion and instinct. Artists, as we saw in the first chapter, are close to dreamers in the sense that they are active collaborators in the extra-ordinary process through which instinct and bodily function are converted into image and phantasy – and herein lies their great educational role. For if there is a formal and reciprocal relationship between image and instinct, it follows that the development of an image can not only release powerful flows of instinctual energy but can also redirect that energy along new routes.

Let me condense part of the main argument into three propositions:

First proposition: that the image making propensity lies at the very heart of our biological nature. Images, we might say, form the first language of humankind. We are taught how to speak, but we are not taught how to dream.

Second proposition: that through conscious collaboration with the unconscious image-making forces (images, in this context, being the symbolic and spontaneous expression of instinct and emotion), we can refine, broaden, and deepen our own natures within the life of culture.

Third proposition: that the arts – which are devoted to the development and re-creation of metaphors – have, therefore, a unique part to play in the elaboration of individual con-sciousness.

James Hillman has written: 'What we do within our imagination is of instinctual significance ... By working on imagination, we are taking part in nature in here.'[2] Idolatry, then, was not perhaps such a perversion of human consciousness! Through a worship of images and ikons people were able to make immediate contact with their own instinctual energies, their own submerged identities, their own dreams. When we look at the metaphoric exuberance of an Indian temple or a Gothic cathedral and we consider our own recent Modernist award-winning architecture, with its glass, steel, and concrete blocks, we cannot but be aware of the nature of our loss, for without a rich plurality of images and ikons we cannot easily locate those inward states of being that the symbols are outer representations of. An environment functional in design tends to make humanity functional in nature. Our inwardness, being unrepresented, becomes difficult to grasp. Paradoxically, in a sterile cement and glass environment we become less than we are. If a house is only 'a machine for living in' (Corbusier) the danger is that the inhabitants of that house become automatons.

Plate 17   A nymph from The Great Stupa in Sanchi 1st Century A.D.
Without a rich plurality of images we cannot easily locate those inward states of being that the symbols are outer representations of.

124

Yet why has metaphor become so neglected as a means of knowledge and understanding? And to what extent can the power of metaphor be demonstrated? These are the questions I want to address in this chapter. I want, first, to indicate some reasons for the inferior status of metaphor in Western civilization and then move to show, in a more positive manner, the actual power of phantasy *to cognize* human reality. I want to affirm the cognitive and creative power of the imaginal, for I believe that if this is recognized the value of the arts will be immediately perceived, and perhaps even a way forward for contemporary art beyond Modernism be discerned.

The Suppression of Metaphor

In the last chapter I attempted to indicate how certain negative features of Western philosophy lead to a general misunderstanding of art and metaphor. Particularly since the Renaissance, philosophers both in the rationalist stream and in the empiricist stream have tended to reject the arts as superficial pursuits, as decorations and diversions rather than powerful and necessary sallies into the hinterland of consciousness. If, as with the rationalists, the world is known only through the categories of pure reason, then it must follow that all the other *dramatis personae* who compete for a hearing in the active theatres of the psyche are judged as 'subjective', 'emotive', 'fantastic', 'illusory', 'unreal', not to be heeded. Hegel saw an inevitable contradiction between the sensuous base of art and the conceptual base of art and in his Platonic maxim 'the Rational is the Real: the Real is the Rational' implicitly judged art as less important and confirmed on a grand scale the bias of Western civilization. If, on the other hand, as with the empiricists, the world is known only through experimental science and if, therefore, the main purpose of philosophy is to cleanse the language so that it can be used more and more clinically and accurately by the scientist, then in this counter-tradition also it can be seen how a similar rejection of the inward life of feeling and imagination developed.

Locke, in his desire for a simple language of sign-object equivalence, attacked metaphor. Hume wanted to commit to the flames all those books devoid of deductive reasoning or experimental reasoning, for lacking such qualities they could only embody 'sophistry and illusion'. Bentham, we are told by John Stuart Mill, held that 'words ... were perverted from their proper office when they were employed in uttering anything but precise logical truth!'[3] James Mill, who was converted to utilitarianism by Bentham and who was responsible for creating one of the most inhuman education programs ever devised, regarded all intense feelings as pathological phenomena. 'For passionate emotions of all sorts, and of everything which has been said or written in exaltation of them, he professed the greatest contempt. He regarded them as a form of madness.'[4] With such a tradition behind it, it is not surprising that in our own century logical positivism made the word 'emotive' a term of abuse and has culminated in a fascination with 'language games' with no interest in what lies beneath the game in the deep preconceptual sources of our being.

It is important to stress that the arguments for imagery are not intended to deny the importance of experimental reasoning or deductive reasoning for in themselves they represent noble achievements; their form and procedures are an essential part of our intellectual heritage and the inherent structure of the mind. The problem is that rational categories have claimed a monopoly in interpretation and have thus excluded other more primitive and existential modes of symbolic elaboration and exploration. There is, perhaps, bound to be a certain tension between imagistic and conceptual forms because the psyche would seem to yearn for unity, and always struggles to reduce the many to the one. The philosopher shouts 'concept', the art-makers, 'image'. Neither heeds the other. The truth would require us to embrace both – yet what can be painlessly expressed in an abstract proposition cannot be converted by incantation into an immediate experience. In life, we seem to work through one dominant mode or the other. We dream in images. We argue in concepts. We strive for a synthesis that invariably eludes us. The challenge is one of accepting in the same existence a plurality of competing forces, to allow both the images and the concepts, to let the bright metaphors and the abstract voices emerge, on their own terms, from the complex and many-faceted psyche. When the images and colours have been banned – and when it can be shown that these have a primary connection with instinct and feeling – then the historical moment has been reached for a defence of the imaginal, but such a defence should entail an attack only on the excesses of reason, the hubris of reason, not on reason itself. Nor should it exclude the necessary and shaping influences of all that is symbolically transmitted in the communal life of the culture, religion and the arts. The true dialectic consists in the tense holding of opposites, not in their exclusion or their integration, but in the hard-won recognition of their necessary differences. We cannot afford to choose between myths and logos.

In the last chapter I explored the nature of the mythological. Here I wish to analyze the revelatory potential of phantasy.

The Case of Dibs

I will take for my examples experiences recorded in autobiography and biography. The first involves the phantasy of a young boy in psycho-therapy. The second is taken from the autobiography of Yvonne Stevenson and records the dramatic experience of a young woman trying to free herself from a highly repressive background. The third example comes from one of my students, who was working on a one-term course that included the task of writing an autobiography. The fourth and last example comes from the remarkable but not widely-known autobiography of Edwin Muir. I have chosen these autobiographies for no better reason than that they were at hand when I began to explore this theme and that, I think, they admirably demon-strate my general thesis. There is no doubt in my mind that many other autobiographies would yield further examples of phantasy in its educative role (as well as its destructive role); indeed, the most unlikely autobiography in this area of phantasy, that of John Stuart Mill, demonstrates the fact that, at times, phantasy (serving the purpose of a creative unconscious) can see deeper and further than that sharpest of agents, the analytical intellect.

The first example, then, is taken from *Dibs: In Search of Self*, a detailed description of a young boy's psychotherapy. Dibs is the son of two distinguished parents; in the published account his father is presented as a renowned scientist, his mother a surgeon. The parents, while well-adapted to the public world of professional work, are in no way adapted to their own emotional natures. They are bitterly disap-pointed with their child, alarmed by his irrationality, depressed by his seeming lack of talent. They are embarrassed, as it were, by his infantilism and even lock him away when their distinguished guests visit them. Although his mother succeeds in teaching him to read at the age of 2 he is regarded as stupid, clumsy, and maladjusted. At 5, although attending a conventional school, Dibs is unable to relate to other children and recoils from his teachers. It is at this point that his psychotherapy begins. A large part of his therapy, a therapy that would seem to have been remarkably successful, consists of playing (for one hour a week under the guidance of Virginia Axline, who is both the psychotherapist and the author of the book) in a sand pit and with a doll's house. In one of the crucial sessions he works out, through the elaboration of phantasy in play, the true nature of his feelings. His phantasy provides a concise image of his own state and includes within it a creative answer. It is an unsophisticated example of the revelatory power of imagery. To understand its nature, it will be necessary to quote a lengthy section from the book.

Dibs has emptied the doll's house of its four dolls, the mother doll, the sister doll, the father doll (who has gone to buy a microscope for his son) and the boy doll (who has gone out 'because he doesn't like the locked doors'). The phantasy continues with the return of the father doll:

Dibs got up and paced the room glancing at me from time to time. Then he knelt down beside the house again and picked up the father doll. 'He called and called to the boy and the boy came running in.' Dibs brought the boy doll back beside the father. 'But the boy ran in so fast he bumped into the table and upset the lamp. The father cried out that the boy was stupid. A stupid, silly, careless boy! "Why did you do that?" he demanded, but the boy wouldn't answer him. The father was very angry and told the boy to go to his room. He said he was a stupid, silly child and he was ashamed of him.'

Dibs was tensed up, immersed in this scene he was playing out. He looked up at me and must have felt that I was as deeply in the experience as he was. 'The boy slipped out of the house and hid', Dibs whispered. 'The father didn't notice what happened. Then ... 'He got up and hurried across the room after the mother doll and brought her back to the house. 'The mother was finished with her park visit and so she came back. The father was still very angry and he told the mother what the stupid boy had done. And the mother said "Oh dear! Oh dear! What is the matter with him?" Then all of a sudden a boy giant came along. He was so big nobody could ever hurt him.' Dibs stood up. 'This giant boy saw the mother and father in the house and he heard what angry things they said. So he decided to teach them a lesson. He went all around the house and he locked every window and every door so they could not get out. They were both locked in.'

He looked up at me. His face was pale and grim. 'You see what is happening?' he said.

'Yes. I see what is happening. The father and mother are locked in the house by the giant boy.'

'Then the father says he is going to smoke his pipe and he gets some matches and he strikes a match and drops it on the floor and the room catches on fire. The house is on fire! The house is on fire! And they cannot get out. They are locked in the house and the fire is burning faster and faster. The little boy sees them in the house where they are locked in and burning and he says "Let them burn! Let them burn!"' Dibs made quick darting snatches at the mother and father doll as though he would save them, but he drew back and shielded his face as though the fire he imagined was very real and burning him as he attempted to save the father and mother.

'They scream and cry and beat on the door. They want to get out. But the house is burning and they are locked in and they can't get out. They scream and cry for help'.

Dibs clasped his hands together and tears streamed down his face. 'I weep! I weep!' he cried to me. 'Because of this I weep!'

'Do you weep because the mother and father are locked in the house and can't get out and the house is burning?' I asked.

'Oh no!' Dibs replied. A sob caught his voice and broke it. He stumbled across the room to me and flung his arms around my neck while he wept bitter tears.

'I weep because I feel again the hurt of doors closed and locked against me,' he sobbed, I put my arm around him.

'You are feeling again the way you used to feel when you were so alone?' I said.

Dibs glanced back at the doll's house. He brushed away his tears and stood there breathing heavily. 'The boy will save them,' he said. He went to the boy doll and took him to the house. 'I'll save you! I'll save you!' he cried. 'I'll unlock the doors and let you out.' And so the little boy unlocked the doors and put the fire out and his father and mother were safe.

He came back to me and touched my hand. He smiled wanly. 'I saved them,' he said, 'I didn't let them get all burned up and hurt.'

'You helped them. You saved them,' I said.

Dibs sat down at the table, staring straight ahead. 'They used to lock me in my room,' he said. 'They don't do it any more, but they used to.'

'They did? But not any more?'

'Not any more,' Dibs said, and a trembling sigh escaped him. 'Papa really did give me a microscope and I have lots of fun with it.' He got up from the table and went across the playroom to the spot where he had put the sister doll. He carried her back to the doll's house and put all four dolls in chairs in the living room.[5]

The metaphor speaks eloquently enough; it enacts faithfully the boy's own emotion, his feelings of anger and bitterness, as well as his ambivalent desires for revenge and reconciliation. Like a dream it would seem to issue spontaneously from some creative integrating force at the centre of the child. Simultaneously it reveals and partially heals. At the end of the hour Dibs even considers relinquishing his comforter, the baby bottle he still needs for emotional sustenance. He said:

'I'm a big boy now. I don't need the baby bottle.'

'You don't need the baby bottle any more?' I commented.

Dibs grinned. 'Unless I sometimes want to be a baby again,' he said. 'However, I feel. However I feel, I will be.'

He spread wide his arms in an expansive gesture. 'Cock-a-doodle-do,' he crowed. 'Cock-a-doodle-do!'

He was relaxed and happy now. When he left the playroom he seemed to leave behind him the sorrowful feelings he had uprooted there.[6]

The phantasy also anticipates the future sequence of events, for Dibs, by insisting on his own feelings and his own core of identity, eventually succeeds in drawing his parents into a recognition not only of him, a 6-year-old child, but also the suppressed and deprived nature of their own phantasy and feeling experiences. His search for self compels them to enter into a relationship where intellect and achievement are not the only criteria for being. 'I saved them,' he said, 'I didn't let them get all burned up and hurt.' In the concluding act of the phantasy Dibs is responsible for returning all four characters, mothers, father, sister, and himself, to 'the living room'. In a sense this is what he was able to do as a result of the phantasy in his actual life. Phantasy can thus anticipate and prepare for 'reality'.

The Case of Yvonne Stevenson

The second example of thinking through imagery is taken from Yvonne Stevenson's autobiography, *Hot-House Plant*. It is a dramatic example. It does not represent the vague if continuous image-making energies of the psyche; rather it shows this natural process brought to a pitch of intensity and to a level of experience one might characterize as visionary. The vision manifests to the psyche all that has been previously ignored, suppressed, undervalued, and negated. But in its very 'abnormality' it points to an innate propensity of the mind to create images charged with inner meaning and the power to heal. Its abnormality points to a normal process of the psyche. Once again, it will be necessary to quote at some length. And we will find, as with the case of Dibs, that the process is largely self-explanatory. The visionary experience comes toward the end of the autobiography as, in many ways, the final act of clarification forcing the author to see the limitations imposed by her restricted childhood (the daughter of a vicar, the pupil of two private single-sex church schools) and to recognize dimensions of human experience other than that of self-sacrificial service and self-immolation. Her whole personality had, in truth, contracted to that of a fierce Puritan conscience. 'I had always' she writes, 'ignored the little voice "I want"'. This process of self-recognition had already begun at the age of 19 when she met another student at college who persuaded her to consider, among other things, 'the unity of opposites'. But intellectual discussion, while opening up, cannot resolve the complex dilemmas of a life divided between the identity that has evolved to meet the past and an identity that has not found itself and yet longs to be itself. Propositions tend to work somewhat outside the bewildering currents of contradictory feeling that flow through a person brought up in one philosophy of abnegation and desirous of another philosophy, more affirmative, more inclusive of self. Such propositions need complementing by a stronger and deeper experience involving body, feeling, and imagination. Such an experience Yvonne Stevenson undergoes and describes in her autobiography.

The visionary passage comes in the autobiographical narrative just after Yvonne Stevenson has related how she had failed miserably her intermediate examinations, examinations in subjects she had never actively chosen but had passively submitted to. She is returning from a walk through the rose gardens, a walk she had made at her mother's suggestions (the 'good' compliant girl again?). During this walk she has found herself loathing the formal perfectionism of the rose garden and also – the outer landscape and the inner mirroring each other – the perfectionism of her own personality:

> And then suddenly it all came to me. A great inner voice boomed at me. 'You have gone wrong TRYING TO BE GOOD and thus breaking the laws of nature.'
>
> The violence of this thought was so great that my legs gave way, and I found myself scrabbling on the ground.
>
> 'Pretend you have lost something', I ordered myself, and I began feverishly turning over the grass.
>
> 'No. People will offer to help. And you look quite mad. Get away from here. Get back to your own room.' I got up and began running.
>
> 'Not so fast. You look quite mad. Everybody will stare.' Grappling with my self-composure, I was suddenly aware that in the sky there was a vision for me to look at, as soon as I could concentrate on it – a vision of my imagination, nevertheless a new 'picture' to study. For picture it was. There seemed to be a gap in the sky, through which I could see dark rumbling clouds pierced by vivid blues and purples. These lowering colours became concentrated into a large, black mass, situated slightly to the right. This I knew was 'God', the real God behind everything – Fate – for across it, in white shining letters, was written 'The Laws of Nature'. It was Nature, then. This black,

seething mass had the shape of an octopus, and one wavy limb was stretched out sideways into the left of the picture. Seated on this black 'paw' of the monster was the Christian Trinity, tiny, shining figures of God the Father, Jesus Christ and the Holy Ghost. With a kind of sneering leer, the black monster crumpled up his paw and they were gone. Then he turned his expression to me, though he had no face, and from behind the white lettering came a voice saying: 'I know of no labels. What I have made I have made. Courage and cowardice, love and jealousy. Cruelty. What you call Good and what you call Bad. To me everything has its place in my scheme. It is sin to break my laws. You have broken the laws of nature. I did not create you to be good. I CREATED YOU AS I CREATED YOU.'[7]

In a state of agitation, compulsively repeating to herself as she walks 'A perfect fool ... a perfect fool ... a perfect fool,' she returns quickly to the solitude of her own college room where the second act of the inward drama begins.

As soon as I was alone forces greater than myself took control of me. I found myself with my hands raised slightly above my head, my eyes closed; and I was squirming my body, shoulders and head sideways as if I were trying to lower myself through a narrow hole. As I 'fell free' (though still standing), I opened my eyes and 'saw' the inner flank of a great, black hairy leg. Gasping with surprise, I twisted my head up and 'saw', towering over me, the legs apart, a huge gorilla-like monster, with a round face and gentle, benign expression. I recognized at once what it represented to me – the evolutionary scale the laws of nature – man's predecessor, the hairy ape. I knew then that I had just fallen from between its legs.

'I have been born again,' I whispered aloud. 'I am part of nature now. A human animal. That means I must join myself up to my body. There must be no longer a division of the neck.' I stepped onto the hearthrug, turned round with my back to the fire, and stood very straight.

'Yes, that's it. I will entrust myself to the laws of nature, since I'm part of nature. And the laws of nature will guide me through my body; they will send me their messages, up through my neck to my head, and I will no longer use my head alone – my reason – and neglect the feelings in my body.'[8]

At this point she pauses, savouring, she writes 'this new sensation which was upon me', this feeling of being 'all of one piece', united. Then, without any sense of choice but rather of submitting to a drama deeper than her highly-developed will power, she is drawn into the third and last act:

> I paused, and for a moment savoured this new sensation that was upon me – that of being joined up at the neck so that I was all of one piece. Suddenly I felt strange forces, like little wires, pulling me forwards and downwards. In a loud voice I said: 'I know what I have to do.' A deep, black pit had appeared before me, and these little wiry forces were urging me to step into it. Once more the blackness represented the laws of nature, my new allegiance. With a kind of joy I said to myself, 'I shall dare to. And since I am a part of nature it's bound to be all right.' I stepped into the air and into the pit. At that I began to have the sensation of slowly falling – down a lighted tunnel.
>
> 'I am like Alice in Wonderland,' I thought, and went on floating down until I suddenly landed in a heap of dry twigs and leaves.
>
> 'Now what do I do? Alice had a white rabbit to guide her!' And then I remembered my new guide. What did my body want to do? It was straining forward, wanting to run – for a long, straight corridor had suddenly appeared before me.
>
> 'I must run and run,' I said to myself and began running along at great speed. And there, at the end of the corridor, no bigger than a tiny speck, was an image of my mother, kneeling down on one knee, with her arms outstretched, shouting to me, 'I love you *whatever* you're like, however naughty you are. Whether you're good or naughty I love you just as much.' I began changing into a smaller and smaller little girl until I was of a size to fit her kneeling height, and was approaching her to within about twenty yards, when suddenly she disappeared and was replaced by a new figure – that of myself at the age of 14, standing to one side and gazing with horror at that group of sixth formers in my first boarding school. The head girl in the centre of the group was saying angrily, 'What she wants is a thorough squashing. To be treated like a new girl ...' The moment when something inside me had snapped as if breaking apart.
>
> 'It is *myself*, it is *myself*, that I must make friends with!' I

cried aloud, and rushed up to that 14-year-old girl. I turned her round to face me and clasped her in my arms, as if I were the mother. Still crying, 'It is myself, it is myself!' I staggered over to the bed and sat down, clutching my own stomach as if clutching myself to myself, I then sat gasping for breath, panting, wet with sweat, wet from head to foot.[9]

The self-realization is immediate, physical, emotional, and conceptual, all inextricably bound and flowing together through one single experience. As she rocks to and fro, with her eyes half-closed, she accuses herself of betrayal. 'Six years! Six years ago I abandoned you. Abandoned my own feelings.' Slowly the outer world, which has been totally eclipsed by the power of her own imagery, acting as if 'out there', projected on the world's face, slowly the outer world returns, almost with a comparable revelatory force because it is a new world that is witnessed.

Then I became aware of the sound of tennis being played in the court below my window. I opened my eyes fully and looked across the room. I had to jam the side of my hand into my mouth to stop myself from screaming. The room looked different! It was three-dimensional and in colour! Before it had always appeared more flat and in a kind of black and grey way. The colours were there, of course, and yet they had not been there, they had not intruded right into my consciousness.[10]

I trust I have quoted enough from *Hot-House Plant* to give the reader a sufficient grasp of Yvonne Stevenson's experience. For a full understanding, of course, the reader must turn to the autobiography itself. I do not want to labour here the manifest/latent content of the dramatic phantasy; I want, rather, to make a number of conceptual points about the actual nature of the phantasy and its educative power.

First, we can see that images represent a preconceptual form of knowing. They possess meaning, a meaning that, in Yvonne Stevenson's case, is very quickly made conceptually apparent: 'In white shining letters was written "The Laws of Nature".'

Second, we can see that phantasy tends to project itself from what we might call 'inner space' to 'outer space'. The images come from out of the sky. The deep black pit is there before her. What is within is experienced as being out there (it is clearly a similar process to that by which mythic images are projected across the face of the universe).

Third, the images, at least at critical moments (such as those of Dibs

135

and Yvonne Stevenson) are not only seen but are actively undergone. The whole body has to encounter them.

Fourth, the kind of knowledge locked within the dramatic sequence of the imagery is existential in character; that is, it reveals a personal truth, not a scientific truth. The gorilla god is not to be given ontological status but psychological meaning for it pertains, first and foremost, to the unique condition of Yvonne Stevenson. Another individual might well need to encounter a numinous god. The truth of imagery is personal in nature, but nonetheless real for that.

Fifth, imagery, being primarily the language of feeling and all those meanings that are accessible only through feeling, is often, in its spontaneous and strange eruptions, serving some deeper purpose, that of selfhood.

The Case of Jacqueline Langlois

I want now to take two examples that may seem more literary, but in being 'literary' it is hoped they will show how close the activity of culture-making invariably is to the indigenous process of the human mind. From the perspective of this chapter, art is the formal and communal elaboration and refinement of all the elusive, dramatic, ever-changing feeling, mood, and phantasmagoria thrown up by the conscious, semiconscious, and unconscious psyche. The arts provide the ritualized forms of feeling, make visible the rhythms of breath and blood, hold up for contemplation the ceaseless imagery of the active imagination; they return us to ourselves not, in essence, changed, but more coherent, more complete, at a higher level of integration. It is for this reason that Susanne Langer asking the questions 'Who knows what feeling is like? Who has a naïve but intimate and expert knowledge of feeling?' answered with the following reply:

> Above all, probably, the people who make its image – artists, whose entire work is the making of forms which express the nature of feeling. Feeling is like the dynamic and rhythmic structures created by artists: artistic form is always the form of felt life, whether of impressions, emotion, overt action, thought, dream or even obscure organic process rising to a high level and going into the psychical phase, perhaps acutely, perhaps barely and vaguely.[11]

In some of the courses at the University of Sussex I ask my students to make an autobiography. I will outline the importance of such work in the next chapter. Here with Susanne Langer's formulation at the front of our minds, I want now to present my third example of thinking through phantasy. Recently, one of the students began to see a way of representing experience other than through the category of historical time. She discovered metaphor. In a letter accompanying her lengthy autobiography, Jacqueline Langlois wrote: 'Poetry is perhaps the most natural expression for autobiography'. She also attempted an analysis of the strengths and weaknesses of her own writing:

> I would like to say a little about how I tried to write, and the different frameworks that entered and started warring with one another.
>
> The first piece was the introductory 'how can I tell you best who I am?' p. 2, which took me a long time, but which I liked. But I wrote it *before* the work was done. It was anticipatory and what happened was that I felt by page 34, when it was getting unspeakably dull, that the following pages just did not live up to its promise. I was all there on p. 2. By p. 4, looking back I can see that I was just manufacturing, not spinning any more. Maybe this is what disturbs me most. My heart is now pulsating from the work, but the work itself lacks a lot of heart, except in patches. Ugh! The whole thing has tired me out!
>
> Writing this introduction was perhaps the best thing. The intensity of my feelings drove my language into metaphor. It was very exciting because the metaphors just took over and I found myself in a different plane of consciousness.
>
> The 'personas' passage that 'ghosts' starts off with immediately wanted to turn itself into poetry and go down into it's own realm instead of moving along into the autobiography elle-même.[12]

'The intensity of my feelings drove my language into metaphor.' The passage 'immediately wanted to turn itself into poetry and go down into its own realm'. Here we find, again, intense feeling manifesting itself not as recall but as metaphor, as a new series of relationships and connections illuminating self and the world in which it lives. As we shall see, in the sequence in which the writer felt 'all there' the self has become part of a myth, the autobiography part of a universal biography.

Here are pages two and three of the autobiography, ending where

137

the subsequent descent into linear rather than mythic time becomes apparent.

How can I tell you best who I am? Each my word an inkling for your portrait. I will give you my soul if you don't lose it. A beautiful piece of work this, but some of the silken threads may have been stolen, I cannot tell.

The real piece of work is spun from my own silk and sometimes it shines with God's own colours, but much is soiled and torn I can't give you this one – it is not in my hands to give. I can only get it when I die. Roll on delivery day!

Sometimes I search for days through the archives, but I can't tell which is the right document. 'Come on' I shout, 'give me back what is mine! Miritrovo nel una selva selvaggia [13] and I can't get out!' The guru at the door says that all the documents used to be filed in the Ancient of Days, but when God was born, the angels around him started to whisper and all the paper blew away. So, now, no-one can find their documents, unless they are very clever.

'That's no good to me! I'm not clever and if I don't get a light for this damn pestilence of vapours [14] soon I am going to get asthma! I mean it!'

To start the weaving of this tapestry, I had first to throw a pebble into a pond. This pebble was an immaculate conception – just the right weight and completely round. I dropped it neatly into the water. But when it touched the water's surface it grew into a huge ragged boulder and waves drove higher than my boat and I felt sick because the horizon had gone.

When the storm had abated I felt much better and the sea was calm, although it is always dangerous.

I was able to consult the ships log:

December 4th 1979 A.D. Vessel launched 4th August 1957. Vessel still intact, although she proved frail in certain adverse circumstances and nearly went down in a bad storm at the beginning of the year, because I hadn't got all the tools to repair the bodywork that had slowly been eroding over the years, particularly the recent years. Luckily, I was able to bring her into port and she was given a major overhaul. She was not seaworthy for six months afterwards ...

... no I wasn't! At least in this I know what it is to be adult. I
know what it is to be suicidal.

When I was little, I was safe. Now I am dangerous.

I am still so uncertain why I cracked up and so aware of
what feel like fundamental weaknesses. [15]

At this point the narrative begins to unpack the metaphor and lay it out.
The autobiography becomes explanatory, rational. The writing enters
the linear mode: *A* then *B* then *C* then *D*. Of course, there is an
important place for such discursive proceedings, but, in this context,
the writer experienced the form as artificial, as distorting and false. It led
to what she described in her own letters as 'a listless chronology', a
documentary recording that, by rendering the surface of experience,
somehow missed its essence, giving the hard husk but not the inner
fruit. How, then, is it that the metaphoric and the poetic have a
meaningfulness not open to faithful factual chronology? Is it that the
individual detail becomes absorbed into a holding archetype? The
ordinary, the trivial, the peculiar is lifted up and, without being negated,
raised onto the high level of symbolic adventure. What might otherwise
have been merely odd now becomes representative, and suffering is
placed in a comprehensive pattern that both contains and supports it.
The phantasy that can spontaneously draw on the rich deposits of the
inherited culture – on *Hamlet* and on Dante, for example – is a phantasy
that not only heals the wounds of the individual but also brings comfort
to that same individual by making the person feel a member of that very
culture, and, through that culture, a member of the human race. Is it this
insight that lies quietly below the suggestion that poetry is the most
natural expression for autobiography?

The Case of Edwin Muir

The last example I want to take is from the poet Edwin Muir's
autobiography. In this undervalued account of his own development as
a person and as a poet, Edwin Muir describes the genesis of one of his
poems. He recalls how one day at the age of 7 he ran away from Freddie
Sinclair, who threatened to fight him. He ran with an excessive sense of
fear ('What I was so afraid of I did not know; it was not Freddie, but
something else; yet I could no more have turned and faced him than I
could have stopped the sun revolving')[16]. And mingled with the fear
was a sense of shame. He felt that everyone in the village could see
his cowardice and his panic: an event and an apprehension common

enough, and yet, as Edwin Muir points out, it took him thirty years to objectify the experience through inherited mythic imagery and in this manner to possess it. Edwin Muir's commentary here is both fascinating in its own right and highly pertinent to our enquiry. He writes:

> I got rid of that terror almost thirty years later in a poem describing Achilles chasing Hector round Troy, in which I pictured Hector returning after his death to run the deadly race over again. In the poem I imagined Hector as noticing with intense, dreamlike precision certain little things, not the huge simplified things which my conscious memory tells me I noticed in my own flight. The story is put in Hector's mouth:

The grasses puff a little dust
Where my footsteps fall,
I cast a shadow as I pass
The little wayside wall.

The strip of grass on either hand
Sparkles in the light,
I only see that little space
To the left and to the right.

And in that space our shadows run
His shadow there and mine
The little knolls, the tossing weeds,
The grasses frail and fine.

> That is how the image came to me, quite spontaneously: I wrote the poem down, almost complete, at one sitting. But I have wondered since whether the intense concentration on little things, seen for a moment as the fugitive fled past them, may not be a deeper memory of that day preserved in a part of the mind which I cannot tap for ordinary purposes. In any case the poem cleared my conscience. I saw that my shame was a fantastically elongated shadow of a childish moment, imperfectly remembered; an untapped part of my mind supplied what my conscious recollection left out, and I could at last see the incident whole by seeing it as happening, on a great and tragic scale, to someone else. After I had written the poem the flight itself was changed, and with that my feelings towards it.[17]

In brief, the original experience of panic and flight is transformed by being imaginatively comprehended through an analogous historically transmitted mythic experience. As the imagery crystallizes so the original feelings are changed. 'I could at last see the incident whole by seeing it as happening, on a great and tragic scale, to someone else.' Through the healing power of metaphor the experience has been truly integrated and transcended. Furthermore, we must note, as with Dibs and Yvonne Stevenson, the imagery is given; it spontaneously arises as a completed *gestalt* to the surface of consciousness, although in Muir's case it derives clearly from the received tradition.

Edwin Muir, reflecting further on the experience, continued:

> I think there must be a mind without our minds which cannot rest until it has worked out, even against our conscious will, the unresolved questions of our past; it brings up these questions when our will is least watchful, in sleep or in moments of intense contemplation. My feeling about the Achilles and Hector poem is not of a suppression suddenly removed, but rather of something which had worked itself out. Such events happen again and again in everyone's life; they may happen in dreams; they always happen unexpectedly, surprising us if we are conscious of them at the time. It is an experience as definite as conviction of sin; it is like a warning from a part of us which we have ignored, and at the same time like an answer to a question which we had not asked, or an unsolicited act of help where no help was known to be. These solutions of the past projected into the present, deliberately announced as if they were a sibylline declaration that life has a meaning, impress me more deeply than any other kind of experience with the conviction that life does have a meaning quite apart from the thousand meanings which the conscious mind attributes to it: an unexpected and yet incontestable meaning which runs in the teeth of ordinary experience, perfectly coherent, yet depending on a different system of connected relations from that by which we consciously live.

The experience points to a creative coordinating energy with its own centre largely beyond the manipulation of the will and often out of the reach of ego-consciousness, that consciousness which has developed in us to meet what we imagine to be the expectations of those who surround us. In ego-consciousness our life exists only in the imagined consciousness of the respected other and, beyond that, in the imagined collectivity of norms, standards, and tacit assumptions. In poetic consciousness, where the energy of dream and metaphor resides, lies the hidden self that longs to exist on terms innate to its own biologically creative condition, yet *within the communal culture* from which it derives most of its own mythic and metaphorical material: its characters, narratives, and numerous images.

In the four examples I have moved from phantasy to poetry, but then, as the last two passages demonstrate, one moves imperceptibly into the other. Emotion, we might say, is the condition for phantasy and phantasy the condition for many of the arts. If Dibs had possessed the technical skill, he could have developed his archetypal phantasy of anger turning into vengeance and vengeance turning into the desire for reconciliation into a powerful play. Indeed, as the use of the words in ordinary language reveals, the play of the child and the play of the dramatist and the play of mind over experience share many characteristic qualities. And Edwin Muir's account of the genesis of his Achilles and Hector ballad reveals that the poetic process and the phantasy process may often be one and the same. The arts do not lie on the far side of life, remote and inaccessible; rather, as it was suggested in the first chapter, they reside at the centre of ordinary existence, being a formal cultural elaboration of deep processes at work in every one. The necessity of art is the necessity of experience or, more precisely, the necessity of the self seeking for its self within the frames of received culture.

There is one last point to be made about metaphor. It cannot be converted into the language of discursive symbolism and retain its transforming energy. Just as water is not H_2O but so much more, so the ikon on the wall is not 'a symbolic figure' for 'religious devotion', so the Achilles and Hector phantasy is not 'a depiction' of 'two archetypal heroes'. *We cannot translate the concrete into the abstract without loss of emotion and inwardness.* To conceptually understand a myth is quite different from the experience of imaginatively living through the same myth. Metaphor is not a clumsy or archaic or precious way of stating a truth that could be expressed more simply through a series of propositions. Metaphor is, on the contrary, a unique and enduring and irreplaceable way of embodying the truths of both our inward and our typical lives. I hope the examples I have given go some way toward establishing this claim.

Conclusion

I have contended that phantasy erupting from the unconscious may, in its more positive manifestations, be serving the needs of the true self. 'It is myself, it is myself, that I must make friends with', concludes Yvonne Stevenson after being dramatically overwhelmed by the images that burst into her guarded consciousness, first in the rose garden, and then in her room. Also, this recognition of self brings with it a recognition of the suppressed elements; in this case, a new valuation of the body, the senses, and the emotions. 'Six years ago I abandoned you. Abandoned my own feelings': the lost is restored to its true place in the hierarchy of being and, even more strangely, the restoration of the suppressed leads to a sudden awareness of the three-dimensionality of the universe and of its extraordinary colour. The phantasy has inaugurated a new and enhanced sense of identity and, at the same time, a heightened consciousness of the surrounding world. When I use the word 'identity' to describe the self I do not mean ego: I mean rather that through such an experience as Yvonne Stevenson describes the brittle, defensive, consciously cultivated ego is broken open and that above its shattered remains a deeper and truer configuration of self emerges. Identity refers to authenticity of self – and it must be quite clear from the examples I have given that the unconscious may well be working for identity more than our daily defensive consciousness, which labours to protect rather than to reveal, to manipulate rather than to be. This is what I take Edwin Muir to mean when in the last passage quoted from his autobiography he declares that life has a meaning quite independent of the conscious meanings claimed for it, a meaning 'which runs in the teeth of ordinary experience, perfectly coherent, yet depending on a different system of connected relations from that by which we consciously live'. It is not a question of being totally passive before the unconscious, but rather of recognizing creative energies in the psyche that are prior to rational conceptualization and of being willing to submit (though not uncritically) to shaping forces operating outside of our analytical reason and our controlling willpower.

We need to ask the question: Is there a formative principle in the psyche transcending social pressures and demanding from us a kind of submission? Is there a force that while not synonymous with instinct is yet deeper than ego, a force for individuation? Is there a self beneath the daily adapted self that longs to be, and whose language comes primarily through image, phantasy, metaphor, dreams and through the collective symbolic inheritance of religion, mythology and the arts? These questions bring us to the theme of the next chapter.

Notes

1. HERMAN, J. (1980) 'Open letter to tract', *Crisis in the Visual Arts, Tract 28*, p. 4.
2. HILLMAN, J. (1972) *Pan and the Nightmare*, Spring Publications, p. 24.
3. MILL, J.S. (1873) *Autobiography*, edited by Signet, p. 55.
4. *Ibid.*
5. AXLINE, V. (1971) *Dibs: In Search of Self*, Penguin, pp. 134–6.
6. *Ibid*, p.137
7. STEVENSON, Y. (1976) *The Hot-House Plant*, Elek/Pemberton, p. 142.
8. *Ibid*, p. 143.
9. *Ibid*, pp 143–4.
10. *Ibid*, p. 144.
11. LANGER, S. (1962) *Mind: An Essay on Human Feeling*, Vol 1, Johns Hopkins University Press, p. 64.
12. Jacqueline Langlois in unpublished autobiography for University of Sussex contextual course.
13. Taken from the first lines of the *Divine Comedy*: 'I found myself in a dark wood.'
14. *Hamlet.*
15. Langlois unpublished autobiography.
16. MUIR, E. (1980) *An Autobiography*, Hogarth Press, p. 42.
17. *Ibid.*, p. 43.
18. *Ibid.*, p. 44.

Chapter 8
Education as Individuation:
The Place of Autobiography

The Psyche is the world's pivot; not only is it the one great condition for the existence of a world at all, it is also an intervention in the existing natural order and no one can say with certainty where this intervention will finally end ... With all the more urgency, then we must emphasise that the smallest alteration in the psychic factor, if it be an alteration of principle, is one of the utmost significance as regards our knowledge of the world and the picture we make it.

Carl Jung

Preamble

In Chapter 4 I argued for a genre approach to the teaching of English and listed autobiography as one of the major genres to be introduced as part of the aesthetic field. In this chapter I want to consider more fully the nature of autobiography, both from a literary and educational viewpoint. I will first outline the historical development of the genre in Western culture, then examine a few of the significant autobiographies of our own century and finally examine some of the inner meanings which can be released through sustained practical work with the genre in the context of education. In particular, I wish to illustrate how autobiography can be the means for that individuation process (within nature, within culture) described in the last chapter.

Introduction

When around 1972 I first became interested in the form and educational uses of autobiography there were few publications concerning its nature or development. Although at the University of Bristol I had studied literature 'from Beowulf to Virginia Woolf', there was virtually no mention of autobiography. I think it would be true to say that the only autobiography widely read by English students was Wordsworth's *Prelude* and that was interpreted essentially as a poem, not as the symbolic recreation of the self in a tradition running back to St. Augustine's *Confessions*. In 1972 the book I recall discovering and the only one recorded in the bibliography of *Autobiography in Education* was Roy Pascal's pioneering study *Design and Truth in Autobiography*. That book had been first published in 1960 and sought to delineate the symbolic field of autobiography and to formulate its distinctive concerns. It is quite extraordinary to consider *now* that as late as 1972 so little had been written on a major form of symbolic enquiry. Yet then, somehow, one accepted the gap. It seemed in the order of things, even if one protested somewhat. Now it seems little short of scandalous because so many academic studies have poured out, particularly from the American university presses, to show the importance of the literary genre and to reveal its structures, its intentions, its history and influence. How could such a major genre pass unnoticed for so long when literature departments flourished in all the major universities? Here it is enough merely to list a few of the studies published since 1980 to indicate the seriousness and scope of the new interest in autobiography:

James Olney (1980) *Autobiography: Essays Theoretical and Critical.*
W.C. Spengemann (1980) *The Forms of Autobiography: Episodes in the History of a Literary Genre.*
David Vincent (1981) *Bread, Knowledge and Freedom: A Study of Nineteenth Century Working Class Autobiography.*
Avrom Fleishman (1982) *Figures of Autobiography: The Language of Self-Writing in Victorian and Modern England.*
Peter Jay (1984) *Being in the Text. Self-Representation from Wordsworth to Roland Barthes.*
Jerome Buckley (1984) *The Turning Key. Autobiography and the Subjective Impulse since 1800.*
Susanna Egan (1984) *Patterns of Experience in Autobiography.*
Linda Peterson (1986) *Victorian Autobiography: The Tradition of Self Interpretation.*

The titles and sub-titles give important clues as to how the genre is being interpreted. Much of the work is structural in character, some of it historical, some of it psychoanalytical. Indeed, there is so much critical work on autobiography being published it is difficult to keep abreast of it. And yet there are serious omissions in the analysis. There is, for example, virtually no sustained work on the uses of autobiography in an aesthetic and educational context or on its development as a contemporary genre. The literary critics are looking backwards and therefore confining themselves to a textual definition of autobiography which in terms of living practice and contemporary consciousness has become somewhat out of key. Yet an historic dimension is, as I have argued throughout this volume, indispensable. Autobiography requires some kind of tradition (even to react against) just as much as creativity. I propose, therefore, to begin with a brief historic overview of autobiography.

The Development of Autobiography in Western Culture

It is pertinent to note that the word 'autobiography' was first employed in 1809 – at the height of the Romantic period – and that the first formal use of the word 'autobiography' in publishing was in 1834 when W. P. Scargill's volume *The Autobiography of a Dissenting Minister* was printed. But the form of autobiography goes back through fourteen centuries to St Augustine's *Confessions* written in the second half of the fourth century. These words, 'autobiography' and 'confessions' – and the particular historical tides on which they bob – are charged with meanings which we must not overlook. The *Confessions* of the Christian period can be viewed from one perspective as the sacrament of confession metamorphosed into literary form; the Autobiographies of the Romantic and Modern periods can thus be understood as those Confessions secularized. In their transformed state acknowledgement (confession derives from the Latin: *confiteri*, to acknowledge) of past failures is made first to the self (not God) and then to the reader (not priest). Confessions, in their traditional form, crave forgiveness: autobiography desires understanding. Confessions are devoted to salvation; autobiographies to individuation.

As with the sacrament of confession so with St Augustine's *Confessions*; it begins with a prayer taken from the tradition, 'Can any praise be worthy of the Lord's Majesty? How magnificent his strength! How inscrutable his wisdom!' The author submits himself to tradition. His opening invocation taken from the Psalms is one of many forming a persistent thread in the tapestry of the highly intertextual writing. He addresses his self-analysis not to himself or to the reader but directly to God.

> My soul is like a house, small for you to enter, but I pray you to enlarge it. It is in ruins, but I ask you to remake it. [1]

The work is a passionate examination and recreation of the author's past before his Maker and Judge; the motivating force comes from the desire for inner renewal. As in the sacrament of confession, the failings of the past are brought consciously to mind in the present for the securing of the future – the quintessential autobiographical rhythm.

Although there were many significant movements in the development of self-reflection and self-recreation between St Augustine and the eighteenth century – in the writings of, for example, Petrarch and Montaigne, or, to take a closely related medium, in the self-portraits of Rembrandt (who all but obsessively recorded himself at every significant stage of his own life) and Durer (who with a new found audacity painted himself in the image of Christ) – it is yet commonly accepted that it was Rousseau who was to take the form of autobiography dramatically further, or, more precisely, to give it its modern

Plate 18 Durer Self-Portrait et 29. *1500.*
This is one of the earliest self-portraits in paint and the most monumental.

Plate 19 Rembrandt Self-Portrait circa 1020.

Plate 20 Rembrandt Self-Portrait *1659.*
Rembrandt painted himself at all the major stages of his life. Put together in chronological
sequence the paintings constitute a visual autobiography of the highest order.

shape. His *Confessions* is a great and original work sounding a new key:

> I have resolved on an enterprise which has no precedent, and which, once complete, will have no imitator. My purpose is to display to my kind a portrait in every way true to nature, and the man I shall portray will be myself.
> Simply myself.[2]

Here lies the character of true *auto*biography, its characteristic mood and predisposition. The writing describes the unfolding life of the unique self (*auto-bios-graphein*). And does so without apology. Even if in the third paragraph there is, as in the confessional manner, reference to 'my Sovereign Judge', the tone is gently mocking and the author – staying firmly at the centre of the stage – retains authority. In Rousseau we find the traditional confessional style transposed into a new key, that of autobiography as a quest for self-definition and for authenticity of being.

After Rousseau the autobiographer addressed himself directly and had for his listener not priest or congregation but the individual reader. The new context, the evolving form, the formation of a more precise word placing the burden on identity, manifested (as did the parallel emergence of the novel) a deepening concern for psychological truth, for the infinitely subtle processes of individuation rather than the definitive once-and-for-all matter of salvation. The number of writers employing autobiography after Rousseau – Goethe, Wordsworth, Herzen, Mill, Ruskin, Tolstoy, Gorki, Gosse, Darwin, Newman – demonstrate that the form had come of age. Our own century and our own times continues to testify to its indispensable place in the act of self-exploration and actualization. As Ronald Duncan put it, in the first sentence of his own autobiography, *All Men are Islands*; 'We settle down to write our life when we no longer know how to live it.'[3] During a period of tremendous confusion in beliefs and values we have evolved autobiography to secure some sense of order and inner identity.

The Analysis of Three Modern Autobiographies

It is not possible to embark here upon a lengthy evaluation of three of the more remarkable autobiographies published in our times: Herbert Read's *The Contrary Experience*, Kathleen Raine's trilogy beginning with *Farewell Happy Fields* and Edwin Muir's *An Autobiography* (referred to in the last chapter). But I bring them together because in literary style and guiding predisposition they seem to me to stand together. They possess the same literary strengths – they are all remarkably eloquent testaments – and they raise simultaneously a cluster of awkward questions about identity and authentic being.

'Perhaps the best autobiography in our language.' So claimed Grahame Greene of Herbert Read's *The Innocent Eye* and, initially, one is tempted only to modify that judgement to 'one of the best'. It is incomparably the best section of *The Contrary Experience*, a volume made up of four discrete autobiographies written at different times and under different circumstances and brought together as late as 1962. *The Innocent Eye* is a precise poetic recreation of Read's childhood memories of his father's farm. There are twelve sections each named after a particular place or object, for example, the Vale, the Green, the Orchard, the Cow Pasture, the Church, the Mill, and each section concentrates on the memories which the place elicits. The book begins with the birth of the writer and ends with the death of his father. The object of the last section is explicitly titled 'Death' and refers also to the death of the child's vision, the termination of his visionary world.

The work has the classical formality of a Baroque concerto. It is free of sentiment. As there is no self-consciousness in the memories, so there is no self-consciousness in the writing. Like Wordsworth's *Prelude* with which it has much in common, it presents the experience of immediate vision, the 'thereness' and 'thatness' of the child's unpremeditated consciousness yet, paradoxically, caught in a language quite beyond the range of the child: the first person singular is used most sparingly for the objects perceived and recreated through the autobiographer's memory define his nature. Where the innocent I is the innocent eye, vision is identity. For Herbert Read such experience is definitive:

> All life is an echo of our first sensations, and we build up our consciousness, our whole mental life, by variations and combinations of these elementary sensations. But it is more complicated than that, for the senses apprehend not only colours and tones and shapes, but also patterns and atmospheres, and our first discovery of these determines the larger patterns and subtler atmosphere for all our subsequent existence.[4]

All the bright moments of ecstasy derive, Read insists, from 'this lost realm'. We progress only to repeat, with less resonance, what has already been given.

But the great bulk of *Contrary Experience* is made up of three other volumes (*The Innocent Eye* comprises only forty pages of a substantial volume). These volumes simply do not possess the same extraordinary power of verbal enactment of the first volume. From a literary point of view *The Contrary Experience* moves from highly condensed expression to conceptual generalization; moves from metaphor to abstraction; from poetic embodiment to the tinkle of 'ideas'. Is it possible that the literary failure is a direct consequence of the informing concept of self which is seen, as it moves away from childhood, to enter exile and unreality? Does the failure of the work to develop cumulatively through time expose a prior failure in a conception of identity which cannot move through time from childhood without diminution? Is it farewell to those happy fields of which, at best, one can only ever capture a dying echo?

The first volume of Kathleen Raine's trilogy, *Farewll Happy Fields* recreates her childhood and adolescence; the second volume, *The Land Unknown* describes her experience as a student at Cambridge University in the thirties, her two short-lived marriages and her various reactions to Positivism, Marxism and Catholicism, all of which she partially embraced only to disown as distorting commitments, distracting her from her own authentic vocation. The third volume, *The Lion's Mouth*, is largely and courageously confined – although that is quite the wrong choice of verb for such a volcanic experience – to the author's attachment to Gavin Maxwell. Of the three volumes *Farewell Happy Fields* is the masterpiece, a sustained piece of autobiographical recreation on a par with *The Innocent Eye*. The language is simultaneously lyrical and precise; it is able to embody the most elusive and haunting of childhood memories:

> A little hand of flame, blue tipped, thin, labile, without sub-
> stance or constant form, dancing gently on a gas-jet from the
> wall. In my warm cot gently laid to sleep I watched those
> luminous fingers dancing for me, for me. I found a song to rise
> and fall with the hand of the flame, glimmer and glum, glimmer
> and glum, glimmer and glum, and so on and on. The living
> flame was a being strange and familiar, familiar and strange. My
> father would turn it out, send the little hand away.[5]

The rhythms there convey exquisitely the mesmerized moment in which object, self and symbol flow together only to disappear out of the stream of consciousness. Kathleen Raine also, but much less frequently, captures the moment of childhood trauma which has its root in the child's spontaneous identification with the world. In the following passage she narrates the death of the bull:

> There was a long waiting; the butcher, alone, crossing the yard,
> gun in hand; a muffled blow, and as in a Greek tragedy the king
> is slain behind the heavy doors of his palace, so we waited for
> the shot, and knew that the great one of our small world, the
> creature of power, had once again been slaughtered; the strong
> by the weak, the great by the small. Presently, as from those
> palace doors, the great body was dragged out of the byre and
> on to the dray, limp and powerless. I saw his pepper-and-salt
> purplish-brown hide with a sense of infinite compassion. I *was*
> him. My body suffered in itself the death of the beast, my skin
> mourning for his skin, my veins for his veins, my five senses for
> his; and when from that anus slipped a mass of faeces, I was
> ashamed for the abasement of his death.[6]

The death of the bull is presented as the death of a god. This, too is
characteristic of Kathleen Raine's instinctive approach. The isolated
event is taken down into its deep archetypal structure and so made
universal. Thus simple places are converted into spiritual conditions –
Ilford becomes Hades, Scotland becomes Paradise, London a kind of
Purgatory ('but now, in London, in order to survive at all,
I must simulate some other person, or perish') – and her journey
becomes, at best, the journey of Everyman. Her life becomes her
'story', her story becomes her 'myth'; her myth, in as much as myth is
always representative, becomes that of our own experience. No sooner
does she name an object than it becomes a symbol of the imaginative
life. And it is here that one is able to identify both the great poetic
strength and the possible existential failing of the trilogy. When the
myth-making propensities of her imagination are converting childhood
memories into a living symbolism – when the childhood experiences
recalled are meeting the needs of the present and leading to transformation and renewal – one feels the essential rhythm of good autobiography. But when she takes her later experience, experience in which she
seems unable to encounter 'the other' even as it gives birth to vision, we
find ourselves, as readers, perplexed. We cannot help asking: is the
vision attained at the expense of self-knowledge? Is the mythic narrative at the expense of the psychological? Does this numinous world of
the imagination depend upon the dissolution of the full impinging
actuality of many diverse worlds which nevertheless come together in
any one experience? Does the predisposition to see self as child-like
visionary innocence inevitably lead to a trilogy which begins with a

literary masterpiece (where childhood is evoked) and yet which, in spite of all its honesty and passion, fails to culminate in any comprehensive significance? Is the author's concept of self adequate to the full task of autobiography.

In Edwin Muir's *An Autobiography* there is a greater sense of growth; there is repetition and return, certainly; but there is also development and integration. The first part, *The Story of the Fable*, was published in 1940 and then incorporated into the complete autobiography first brought out in 1954. The autobiography takes us in chronological order through Muir's childhood in the Orkneys, his experience as an adolescent and young man in Glasgow and Fairport; it narrates his activities and relationships as an emerging writer, in London, Prague, Dresden, Helleran, Italy, Austria, France, Prague again (this time under a Communist regime), and lastly in Rome, where his commitment to Christianity finally crystallizes. The places are important because they mark the stations of an inner journey. Rather like Ilford in Kathleen Raine's *Farewell Happy Fields*, so Fairport (where Muir works in a bone factory of unbelievable squalor) represents the negation of all positives. In Virginia Woolf's terms Fairport symbolizes Non-Being – and in its hideous machinery Muir is tragically entangled for many years. The Orkneys symbolize a prior Eden before Fairport. The two visits to Prague, in part, represent two versions of politics, the liberal and the totalitarian, the open and the closed. While, at one level, the reflection takes the reader deep into archetypal structures – into 'the fable' and those moments of being 'liberated from the order of time' – it is open, at another level, to the fact of historical and biological process, of relationship and social obligation. Individual being is seen as the reel on which the radically different strands of life are wound. There is both a sense of exile (therefore a movement backwards) and a sense of indivisible unfolding (with a forward motion) and such a dialectic allows for individual growth and pain and anguish.

The opening chapter of *An Autobiography*, describing Orkney, has an all but visionary intensity. The reader is gently taken through a sequence of vast still-life images, of childhood memories which have become primordial. The incidents remembered have become so slowed down they imperceptibly slip into a kind of eternity. The power of the writing depends on paragraphs rather than sentences but the following account, describing his father sowing seeds in the spring is characteristic:

I would sit watching him, my eyes caught now and then by

some ship passing so slowly against the black hills that it seemed to be stationary, though when my attention returned to it again I saw with wonder that it had moved. The sun shone, the black field glittered, my father strode on, his arms slowly swinging, the fan-shaped cast of grain gleamed as it fell and fell again; the row of meal coloured sacks stood like squat monuments in the field.[7]

These childhood images were later to form the primary material of Muir's poetry:

A little island was not too big for a child to see in it an image of life; land and sea and sky, good and evil, happiness and grief, life and death discovered themselves to me there; and the landscape was so simple that it made these things simple too.[8]

Yet it is a measure of Muir's growth as a poet and as a man that he is able to employ the childhood images to convey not the world of a child but the hidden import of the most catastrophic events of our era (as, for example, in his great poem *The Horses*) It is also to be observed that Muir's imagination is as capable of presenting the experience of unreality and nausea as of glory and innocence. His chapters on Glasgow and Fairport are so disturbing to read for they recreate, in the way that Herbert Read's War Diary in the *Contrary Experience* fails to, the weird phenomena of dislocation and psychic disease. In fact, Muir has an all but frightening ability to define with a poetic precision the lineaments of pure emotional states. He is the William Blake of autobiography.

His comprehension of depth and complexity is further recorded in his attention to dreams. Should the autobiographer present the streaming images of the unconscious as well as the events and circumstances of everyday experience? Muir writes:

It is clear ... that no autobiography can confine itself to conscious life and that sleep, in which we pass a third of our existence, is a mode of experience, and our dreams a part of reality. In themselves our conscious lives may not be particularly interesting. But what we are not and can never be, our fable, seems to me inconceivably interesting.[9]

For this reason Muir describes more dreams in his autobiography than any other I have read, even Jung's. But surface and underground are not forced to inhabit the same level; they are allowed to co-exist. The fable is not the life; mythic time is not historic time. These very distinctions, I believe, make possible a development and comprehensiveness missing in the other autobiographies. Yet, they in turn create their problems. For where is the self which would mediate between the diverse and distinguished world? And how can the nature of that self be known when many of its truths are out of reach, for much of the time, in the darkness of the unconscious? There are only fragments, memories, elusive movements and 'in a great number of dreams ... a few glints of immortality'.

To consider the three autobiographies together is to detect certain similarities. The writers belong to the same generation; they are poets; they have deep roots not in the urban but in the rural order; they suffer exile; they leave their social class and background; they devote their lives, in different ways, to the truths of the imagination. In their autobiographies, at least in their most memorable and haunting sequences, one becomes aware of the common quality of the language which, while it remains wholly contemporary, still has behind it the gravity and grandeur of the Authorized Bible and the sinew and pulse of Shakespeare. They also have that unusual power to lift ordinary experience up into the symbolic dimension where it is given an enduring significance, becomes, in Muir's phrase, part of the fable. At the same time, they present the reader with concepts of self which require the most delicate scrutiny. In the case of Herbert Read and Kathleen Raine we find the image of the visionary child which lies deep in the Romantic tradition, yet can the child ever act as metaphor for comprehensive existence? I have suggested that the comparative failure of their work to accumulate, to grow, to deepen, indicates not, in the first place, a literary failure, but a partiality of conception which derives from an inability to fully integrate the human dialectic and the appalling complexity of existence. In Edwin Muir's autobiography we find a similar commitment to what he called the child's 'original vision of the world'. But, at the same time, there is an authoritative recognition of its opposite state; a tacit appreciation of the role of negative experience in the ecology of consciousness. Hence *An Autobiography* has a forward movement. The book develops as the author develops.

The problem which Muir's work raises relates to his persistent sense of the elusiveness and uncertainty of identity. The central preoccupation of autobiography with realization of self is cast into doubt. Perhaps identity is only ever a partial fragment of something larger and, forever, unknowable? Muir states emphatically: 'I can never know myself.' We are always and forever more than we can symbolically grasp. Such a view could be taken to define the limitations of the form. Alternatively, it could be seen as a further challenge to the dominant convention in autobiography in its use of the chronological and historical narrative. Is it not possible to write an autobiography which captures the truth of experience, with its uncertainties, gaps, aspirations, visions and banalities, without relying on the method of linear chronology? Does this hint at the next development in autobiographical recreation? If so, Muir's autobiography, with its sense of human life camped precariously on the border between the ordinary and the fabulous takes us, at points, very close to the new ground. Muir, at any rate, leaves us with the sense that self-knowledge must serve something other than itself. In this deep insight, autobiography, once again, finds its ontological sources; moves us deftly from the certainty of knowledge into the mystery of being.

The Educational Implications of Autobiography

In an educational context the student can be brought into the field of autobiography through being set the aesthetic and personal task of making an autobiography. This can take many forms; not only the traditional form of written narrative but also film, video, photography, dance, drama, montage, painting etc. Some of these forms positively invite a freer method of self-narration, self-figuration and self-presentation. These forms can and do react within the field of established autobiography and often enable the student to find aesthetic shape for distinctive individual experience and elusive memory; and in the reciprocal movement between the emergent self and the expressive symbol further cognitive understanding is invariably developed. I would like now to show the kind of interior development which can take place by reference to one example, the case of the undergraduate student, Rachel Ashman.

The Case of Rachel Ashman

In the spring term of 1983, Rachel Ashman, a student majoring in geography, joined a group of nine other undergraduates to study autobiography. During that term we studied the autobiographies of Edmund Gosse, Maxim Gorki, Carl Jung, Jean-Paul Sartre and Simone de Beauvoir. As we shall see the autobiography of Jung was to exert a powerful influence on Rachel. In the first session I made it clear that in our work there would be three formal tasks:

(i)   The keeping of an experiential journal;
(ii) a sustained experiment in the making of autobiography;
(iii) an essay exploring conceptually some aspect of the work.

I then emphasized that their autobiography could be *made* in any medium and it was agreed that the fourth seminar should be given over to the presentation of their own work. It was at this fourth seminar that I became aware of Rachel's inner work. Introducing the pile of images on cut-out paper in front of her, she explained that she had enjoyed a particularly close relationship with her grandfather who was now suffering from senile dementia. For her autobiographical work she had decided to consider her relationship with her grandfather and had collected together many photographs which pictured both herself and her grandfather. She had then realized that some of the very early snaps recorded events she could not remember. But now, as her grandfather had lost his memory, the event had disappeared. Where was the event if there was no memory to recall it, recreate it? It was dead. Rachel wrote:

> ... the photographs show two people who cannot testify to their significance. A tension developed between the loss of childhood and fear of death. [10]

A loss of memory represented a threat to her identity. It was in response to this anxiety that she found herself placing the photographs inside her own simple schematic drawings of tombs, crosses and graveyards. Rachel was insistent that this impulse 'took her'; it was not a rational decision. She accused herself of being 'unhealthily morbid', yet pointed out that the action had an inherent momentum of its own and seemed so 'right' that she had continued with it.

At the seminar she handed round the large paper crosses and tombstones in which the photographs of herself and her grandfather had been neatly placed. Rachel subsequently wrote:

> The fact that I too was in the graveyard emphasized the notion that an important part of myself was defined in my relationship with grandad. People are what interactions with others make them. When that source of definition dies so too does a part of your identity. This seems to me the greatest test of the concept of self because the way in which grief is handled is a reflection of

the 'residual' which exists after a definition has died. That residual is you ...[11]

Here, then was one cluster of elements: of childhood, death, failure of memory, grandfather. And against them, but growing out of them, another set: identity, life, autobiography, reflection, Rachel. She wrote:

I have learnt I am burying a conception of myself which could not exist without grandad, yet what is 'left' is me.[12]

At this point, another spontaneous event took place. Rachel *found herself* writing the following epitaph and placing it inside the shape of a large traditional gravestone. At the seminar, apologizing for its 'poetic badness' and its banal rhyming system, she read it out to the group:

GRANDAD
What *will* I remember and what *should* I recall?
   I don't know where to start
Because I have never had to face death before.
   The death of his memory has been curious
     As it means *I* am now
Custodian of the life that *was* between us.

Our past is secured when I hear the words he said,
   Grandad is still alive
Yet, I know in my heart that something is dead.
   I think now I see what I had not understood
     By thinking of Grandad
I am mourning the departure of my childhood.[13]

Rachel later explained what had happened in her discursive essay:

The process of writing an epitaph was frightening because I had not intended to do it... The responsibility which grandad's loss of memory placed on me indicated that far from undermining my importance as a 'separate' self it enlarged and reinforced its existence. As sole 'custodian of the life that was between us' my memory had been given a particular job to do which it had lacked before. I did not realize this until I had got to the end of the epitaph.[14]

The last line brings the awareness that it is her childhood that is also dying and out of this death, for Rachel, comes the birth of the self. For 'the residual' which remains after the childhood relationship, she insists, 'is selfhood'.

The next stage in Rachel's autobiographical journey came with a dream:

> The dream itself was obviously provoked by my mental concentration on the notion of death. I saw a figure of death draped in a long, dark cloak standing next to my bed. The image in itself seems a rather contrived response, almost an expected reaction to my conscious thoughts. However, the vital element in this dream was that the figure was only there when I opened my eyes. He vanished when I closed them. I had to turn my head to the wall to make 'him' disappear. [15]

Baffled by the phenomenon, though still in the dream, Rachel wanted to check whether her eyes were open and looked for the alarm clock by the bedside table. It was there faithfully recording the time between two and half-past-two. In the dream she recalled gazing backwards and forwards from the face of the clock to the figure of death:

> The dream was not just a visual experience. There was a sharp pain running from my neck up through the right hand side of my head. This did not surprise me because the sensation is frequent but its significance was alarming. It meant that it was difficult to turn my head away from the figure due to the stiffness in my neck. The entire episode completely disappeared when I went back to sleep. [16]

Rachel felt that her dream was conveying an insight which could not be easily formulated by language. She decided to make a simple drawing of the dream figure of death and then found herself making a second drawing bringing the clock and the cloaked figure into explicit relationship. She wrote:

> The second drawing was impulsive in its form. I suddenly 'knew' that the figure of death should be holding the clock although this had not actually been the case in the original experience. I had not seen the figure's hands but the drawing seemed to demand that he should be holding 'time'. I realized that this impulse to allow death to be in control of time was an important step in my reflections. Another idea had been unfolded through the use of images and dreams. [17]

In placing the time of the clock and the figure of death together, Rachel had created room for an alternative formulation of the nature of inner experience in relationship to time:

The division between life and death assumed by the clock ignores the crucial instrument of the mind in defining a life. The mind induces memory as a means of providing a continuity of experience which can be called life. Each episode is related to others through the medium of the mind. Meanings are given to activities and relationships. It fosters identity. This constitutive element of life is all important. It should therefore be argued that when it ceased to operate then 'life' is no more in terms of capacity to relate experiences to each other. Grandad is not dead according to the clock monitoring his physical activity. Yet a death has already taken place, an event which the clock and its concept of time fails to recognize. [18]

Rachel continued to explore her preoccupation with time by cutting out clock faces and superimposing images of her own life over the mechanical numbers. The images of felt and valued experiences were being put literally above the linear sequential figures of abstract time.

My own reflections have introduced me to the idea that once the implications of time have been questioned those concepts such as death and childhood which rely on them become volatile. It is this lucidity and conceptual freedom which made me realise that what appear to be mutually hostile notions can be reconciled. It also led me to be more aware of the power of impulses, dreams and images to act as a check on the blindness of consciousness and its assumptions. [19]

In Rachel's autobiographical work during that spring term we detect a development which cannot be easily categorized, in which paradoxes dissolve into new thoughts and new thoughts suggest further divisions which, in turn, give birth to further unifying insights. 'The Dynamism', as she put it herself, 'behind the recollections was based on the way in which the contradictory concepts on one particular thought were reconciled in the following event'. She uses the word 'event' because it conveys the dramatic nature of the knowing. An inner play is being performed. 'I felt myself', she wrote, 'to be a spectator in an audience rather than an actor in the performance.' It is significant to note, also, that the intellectual discovery seemed 'to be possible with the use of a medium other than conventional language in the form of sentences'. The collecting of photographs, the placing of them in gravestones, the dream, the elaboration of the dream through two drawings, the placing of photographs inside clock faces; many of the major moments in the autobiographical journey are marked by first spontaneous and then reflective encounters with imagery. The last two sentences of her long analytic account read as follows: 'Writing has helped to clarify and order thought. It has helped me to feel cleansed.'[20] Timothy Towers has described the major concern of making autobiography as 'a redemption of time past through sifting it for its meanings for our contemporary existence.'[21] It aptly summarizes Rachel's autobiographical work. Responding to her experience we sense a formative process at work, at once intellectual and emotional, conscious and unconscious, objective and deeply personal. Through a variety of symbolic modes (through writing, reading, photography, drawing, dreaming, collage-work) she searches for a multiplicity of intersecting meanings (of childhood, of relationships, of memory, identity, time and death) which make sense of her contemporary existence. This is educational work of the first order, and, it is also expressive and creative work, an art process in its own right: the art of autobiography.

Areas for Further Study in Autobiography

It remains to suggest a few areas which require further study and reflection. I will do this by raising clusters of questions around different facets of the autobiographical enterprise. I will not attempt to answer my own questions; they exist to provoke, to excite and invite further acts of creative analysis and educational innovation.

Firstly, we need to consider the ways in which the study and making of autobiography can be developed in our classrooms
What forms of genre, at what age, can be effectively introduced?
What telling examples can be located for children? For adolescents?
In what structural ways can pupils be guided in their making of autobiography?
How can work based on family-albums and photographs be developed further?
What work can be developed with film, dance, art, drama, mime, music?
Does autobiography provide one *locus* for interdisciplinary work between the arts? Between the arts and the humanities?

Secondly, we need to examine other contexts for the development of autobiography.
Could it be used more extensively in the training of teachers and in various in-service courses for teachers?

Could autobiographical work be included in the educational programme offered to, say, prisoners or delinquent adolescents in special institutions?

Could it be adapted for use in the training courses of probation officers, social workers, nurses, doctors, etc.?

What are the connections between the 'talking-cure', psycho-drama, *gestalt* work and autobiography?

Can the making of autobiography be adapted for use in personal therapy? Or is the therapy already a mode of autobiography?

Thirdly, we need more discursive studies of the field of autobiography.

Is the self-portrait in painting the equivalent to autobiography in literature?

Have we a language for 'reading' the self-portrait? (There is no seminal study of the self-portrait as yet.)

What are the corresponding forms (if any) in all the other arts?

What do current self-representations tell us about our dominant concept of self?

What is the place of narrative in the personal telling of life?

Where do the narratives for our own personal narrative come from?

What are the various analogues for the depiction of the self?

Fourthly, we need to examine further the use of autobiography as a method of intellectual analysis.

To what extent can autobiography be directly used as a tool of research?

Does Sheila MacLeod's *The Art of Starvation*, which examines the phenomenon of *anorexia nervosa* through the author's experience of it, offer a model for such work?

Does Ronald Fraser's *In Search of a Past*, by mixing 'objective' documentary and 'subjective' autobiography, also offer a structure and method which allows for a complex dialectic between object and subject, between history and self-narration, and thereby offer a paradigm for critical investigation?

To what extent do the autobiographies of some of the feminists (for example, Robin Morgan's *The Anatomy of Freedom* and Ann Oakley's *Taking it like a Woman*) impinge on this issue by consciously demonstrating the connections between the self and the world, between the self and academic knowledge?

What, in brief, is the relationship between autobiography and knowledge? And what are the implications of this on methods of research?

Questions! Too many questions, listed too indiscriminately. But I have decided to let them stand virtually unedited to indicate much that remains to be done. If we also realize that behind most of the questions lurk *further assumptions about the self and the nature of experience that need questioning*, we can see that the field remains vast and problematic.

Sometimes, in a tired civilization like our own, it seems that there is nothing left to pursue, that we can only repeat, with less resonance, what others have said definitively before us. Autobiography, however, is an area which has been largely ignored and positively invites fresh acts of imaginative and intellectual attention.

Notes

1. ST. AUGUSTINE *Confessions*, trs. by R.S. Pine Coffin, Penguin (1961), p. 24.
2. JEAN JACQUES ROUSSEAU *Confessions*, trs. by J.M. Cohen, Penguin (1953), p. 17.
3. DUNCAN, R. (1964) *All Men are Islands*, Hart Davis, p. 9.
4. READ, H. (1962) *The Contrary Experience*, Secker & Warburg.
5. RAINE, K. (1973) *Farewell Happy Fields*, Hamish Hamilton, p. 12.
6. *Ibid*, p. 6.
7. MUIR, E. (1980) *An Autobiography*, Hogarth Press.
8. *Ibid*.
9. *Ibid*.
10. From the written work of Rachel Ashman at the University of Sussex, Spring term 1983.
11. *Ibid*.
12. *Ibid*.
13. *Ibid*.
14. *Ibid*.
15. *Ibid*.
16. *Ibid*.
17. *Ibid*.
18. *Ibid*.
19. *Ibid*.
20. *Ibid*.
21. TOWERS, T. (1986) *Autobiography and Education*, (University of Sussex Occasional paper No. 13).

Chapter 9
Towards a Conservationist Aesthetic in Education: A Concluding Manifesto with a New Ecological Note

So, too, at this one moment of time I can feel consciousness stretching from the crystal-line virus that blights tomato plants, through fish, reptiles and mammals to the minds of men. Indeed, it is obviously only an expedient convention to stop with the forms of life that are earliest in time, or the simplest in space. Consciousness must surely be traced back to the rocks – the rocks which have been here since life began and so make a meeting place for the roots of life in time and space, the earliest and the simplest. Why, indeed, stop with this planet? Even if nothing like the human psyche and intellect have developed elsewhere, it is necessary in an indivisible universe to believe that the principle of consciousness must extend everywhere. Even now I imagine that I can feel all the particles of the universe nourishing my consciousness just as my consciousness informs all the particles of the universe.

Jacquetta Hawkes in *A Land*.

Preamble

At the present time we are witnessing in the arts a profound conservationism of mood and disposition. *Not* Conservatism, but conservationism. This conservationism can be seen most dramatically at work in the visual arts; it is recorded, for example, in the marked return to figurative, narrative and landscape painting (at the moment of writing there is a major exhibition of Lucian Freud at the Hayward Gallery and a major exhibition of David Bomberg at the Tate); it is manifested in the sudden flowering of Post-Modernist architecture which relates build-

165

ings to their historic and natural environments, to their communities, and to the inherited grammar of architectural forms; and it is being given propositional clarity in such organs as *Modern Painters*[1] and in the writings of such influential critics as Peter Fuller,[2] Mordaunt Crook[3] and Roger Scruton.[4]

A similar spirit can be observed in drama, dance, music, literature and even film (as it becomes aware of its own eventful history, its quickly evolving conventions and techniques, its own canon of great works). In all of the arts one senses a common desire to reanimate the many variegated traditions eclipsed by the dazzling glare of the Modernist movement. The art-maker, art-critic, art-teacher have become, in part, earnest ecologists, determined to save threatened symbolic forms from extinction. For like the ecologist they know these forms are necessary to the vitality of the whole culture. It is now widely assumed in the general arts debate that the greater the plurality of expressive forms the greater the chances of true creativity.[5] No longer in the arts is it a question of manically asserting one's individual freedom, one's special uniqueness, one's startling originality; it has become more a question of establishing a continuous symbolic community, of returning to sources, of re-establishing vital connections to the historic past as well as to the natural order.

As this emerging conservationist aesthetic is a reaction to the extremes of Modernism, I want first to analyze, however sketchily, that movement. I want, then, to briefly consider some of the implications of my argument for the arts in education, with a particular eye to ecological and environmental issues.

At the outset I must stress that the developments outlined here are already in motion. A remarkable change in the structure of our sensibilities is taking place. It is recording itself most dramatically in the arts. My task is to name the informing conceptions, to delineate their implications, to think them through into fitting educational policies and better teaching methods. As I see it, the emerging conservationism is not only intent on reclaiming the neglected traditions of the past, it is also engaged with a philosophical conception of man and woman as intentional and symbolic beings within the manifold of nature. 'Culture', writes the philosophical biologist Mary Midgley, 'is the completion of instinct'.[6] That is exactly the notion of conservationist aesthetics! Culture is the outgrowth, the articulate culmination of our biological nature and consequently reflects within its forms and rhythms the natural history of all things. Art-making, at root, is thus neither the distorting sublimation of libido (as Freud contended) nor is it a secondary and symptomatic expression of economic forces (as Marx explained) but rather it is a primary and transformative energy of our own nature within Nature, an activity we delight in and need to engage in for a full realization of our creative species. What is involved here is a biological grounding of mental and symbolic activity. Too many philosophers from Plato onwards have put mind on the other side of nature, thus making it alien; and too many, especially in the Empiricist tradition, have rendered the arts a secondary and essentially a trivial pursuit. The biological grounding of symbolic life returns art to the order of nature and makes it fundamental.

The Conservationist Aesthetic and Modernism

The two central strands of the emerging conservationist aesthetic can be discerned powerfully at work in the best of Post-Modernist (or, as Mordaunt Crook prefers to call it, Post-functionalist[7]) architecture. The following account, emphasizing both the historic and the ecological dimensions, brings this out well:

> Critical Regionalism necessarily involves a more directly dialec-
> tical relation with nature than the more abstract, formal tradi-
> tions of modern avant-garde architecture allow. It is self-
> evident that the tabula rasa tendency of modernization favours
> the optimum use of earth-moving equipment ... The bulldozing
> of an irregular topography into a flat site is clearly a technocratic
> gesture which aspires to a condition of absolute placelessness,
> whereas the terracing of the same site to receive the stepped
> form of a building is an engagement in the act of 'cultivating'
> the site. It is possible to argue that in this last instance *the specific*
> *culture of the region – that is to say, its history in both a geological and*
> *agricultural sense – becomes inscribed into the form and realization of the*
> *work.* This inscription, which arises out of 'in-laying' the
> building into the site, has many levels of significance, for it has a
> capacity to embody, in built form the prehistory of the place, its
> archeological past and its subsequent cultivation and transform-
> ation across time. Through this layering into the site the
> idiosyncrasies of place find their expression without falling into
> sentimentality.[8]

Post-Modernist architecture is architecture which honours memory and the specificity of culture and place. In clarifying his conceptions, the

167

above writer refers to a conflict between what he characterizes as 'universal civilization' and 'autochthonous culture'. His concept of 'universal civilization', as abstract, rational, pure, is very close to our own concept of the dominant Modernist spirit to which I would now like to turn. What, then, *was* Modernism?

As a general orientation of the European mind it can be understood best, perhaps, as the formal rejection of the past (both biological and cultural) as offering any substantial guidance to the living of life.

It can be seen as simultaneously emerging from, and marking the end of, the Renaissance. Arguably, it reached its zenith at the beginning of our own century and has begun to disintegrate in our own lifetime. Descartes can be considered in his mode of philosophy, if not in the practice of his life, as the first Modernist. Sitting alone at his stove or fingering the wax on his desk, analyzing the unreliability of his own sense data, Descartes desired a complete illumination into the fundamental structure of things, with no guide, no previous model and no reference back to the accumulated traditions of thinking. His self-imposed and solitary task compelled him to disown as a matter of method all historic culture as well as his own biological nature. In terms of *time* his programme entailed the virtual annihilation of the past tense. That orientation, expressed in innumerable philosophies and further empowered by the growth of science and technology, has remained the dominant orientation of Western culture ever since. To be 'backward-

Plate 21   Modernist Architecture. Le Corbusier L'Unite d'Habitation *at Marseilles.*

Plate 22 Post-Modernist Architecture. The building Marcopolo in London. Post-Modernist architecture honours memory.

Plate 23 Post-Modernist architecture. The new Law Courts in Lewes, Sussex (background) are intimately related to the nineteenth-century Fitzroy Library (foreground). The vital historic element of the location is acknowledged and quoted in the new building.

looking' in our culture is, indeed, to commit a grievous crime against those two validating tenses: time present and time future. Consider, for example, two of the influential formulations of our own century; Walter Gropius' 'start from zero' and Jean Paul Sartre's 'existence precedes essence' (further clarified by 'there is no human nature' and 'to begin with he (man) is nothing'). Both share the same premise: the individual must begin *ex nihilo*, with nothing behind him historically, and with nothing conferred biologically. Modernism always desired to start from the blank slate, the *tabula rasa*, the white sheet. The essential conceptual continuity between the French philosophers Descartes and Sartre is extraordinary and further testifies to the long intellectual span of Modernism. In fact, it is an immense irony that Modernism, in spite of the rhetoric, constitutes a tradition: a tradition to end all traditions.

Modernism in the arts came long after Descartes. Most critics agree that it was a development of Romanticism, establishing itself around the middle of the nineteenth century and reaching its peak in the first decades of the twentieth century. Jungen Habermas defines this immensely complex phenomenon as follows:

> In the course of the nineteenth century, there emerged out of this romantic spirit that radicalized consciousness of modernity which freed itself from all specific historical ties. This most recent Modernism simply makes an abstract opposition between tradition and the present; and we are, in a way, still the contemporaries of that kind of aesthetic modernity which first appeared in the midst of the nineteenth century. Since then, the distinguished mark of works which count as modern is 'the new' which will be overcome and made obsolete through the novelty of the next style.[9]

Aesthetic modernity, then, is also built on the notion of a radical discontinuity, on a self-conscious disruption of time's three tenses. An authentically modern work had to be 'of the moment', had to arrive, as it were, certified as being uncorrupted by the influence of past art. The very term *avant-garde* (at the vanguard, leading the time) tells us a great deal about the characteristic disposition of Aesthetic Modernism.

Such a disposition had to lead, sooner or later, to outer symbolic depletion and inner psychic exhaustion. By the law of its own premises aesthetic Modernism was doomed to extinction. The obsession, in the fifty years between 1930 and 1980, with artistic revolution, with strident change, with endless experimentation (more and more dislocated from the enriching sources of the past) had to culminate in visual gimmickry, dependence on counterfeit commercial iconography and a self-fulfilling minimalism. There are many fallacies in Aesthetic Modernism but the most notable is that of *historicism*[10] in Karl Popper's sense. This fallacy involved the substitution of illegitimate categories for the evaluation and understanding of art. Art came to be no longer widely judged by its intrinsic aesthetic qualities but by its overt relationship to 'modern time'. Thus critics asked of a painting: Was it an advance on the last style? Did it 'go beyond' the nineteenth century, beyond Cubism, beyond Fauvism, beyond Abstract Expressionism, beyond Pop or whatever the last movement was deemed to be? Was it 'relevant'? Did it encode a message for the age? But all of these questions demonstrate a by-passing of the essential primary question: the aesthetic power of the work in its own right, in its own rich field of execution and expression. They all reveal an obsession with the temporary moment.

During the 1970s a desperate cant filled a growing sense of emptiness; by the middle of the 1980s the game was well and truly up. The architecture changed, as did the painters being exhibited in the major public galleries. There was a return to figurative and narrative painting. The Pre-Raphaelites were exhibited at the Tate Gallery, followed by Edward Hopper, John Piper and Francis Bacon. The Hayward Gallery (that hideous temple to functional Modernism) showed the landscape and narrative paintings of Edwin Burra; the Barbican displayed the work of Gwen John and then the work of the Neo-Romantics. All that the spirit of Modernism had repressed and negated was being rediscovered. The importance of the past tense was reaffirmed, as were the value of place, locality, community, ritual, myth, natural materials, ornamentation, beauty, and the numinous. The extremities of Modernism had brought to birth a conservationist aesthetic.

The Teaching of the Arts After Modernism

How does this conservationist aesthetic relate to the teaching of the arts?

To begin to answer this question, it is necessary to examine our key word 'aesthetic' and to relate it to the biological notion of mind referred to earlier. 'Aesthetic' is often taken to denote something akin to refined, exquisite, 'arty' and is tinged with connotations of indulgence, excess, decadence (it is as if the Pre-Raphaelites and the Bloomsbury group had together sealed the word in amber). This, however, is not the use of the word intended here. By aesthetic, in contrast, we denote a kind of bodily knowledge, *an apprehension of patterns through the power of sensibility*, especially as it is formally expressed and developed through all the arts. Our definition honours the etymological root of the word (the original Greek *aisthetika* means *things perceptible through the senses*) as it also sustains the philosophical import of the word developed by Kant. For Kant, aesthetic response entailed an act of sensuous contemplation in which *meanings* were disclosed. These meanings were perceptual in kind, as opposed to conceptual, but, nonetheless, ordered, moving and significant. Put more dynamically we could say that the aesthetic is one of the great modalities through which we symbolically discover and extend our nature within nature.

Thus we find ourselves not only engaged with the biological grounding of mind, but also with a major expansion in our concept of intelligence and rationality. As Howard Gardner claimed in his recent book *Frames of Mind* (subtitled *The Theory of Multiple Intelligences*) the idea of the plural form of intelligence is an idea whose time has come. His argument that there are different modes of rationality, relatively autonomous and innate proclivities of the mind needing, from the cultural environment, continuous sustenance for their fulfilment, is close to our own. But in this book I am anxious to stress the nature and value of aesthetic intelligence. Aesthetic intelligence is perceptual intelligence; it is nurtured and articulated, principally, through the major arts disciplines. Artists, we might say, are perceptual philosophers. Such an insight is crucial to the conservationist aesthetic I am trying to map. It is indicative that the most recent influential books on arts education – Robert Witkin's *The Intelligence of Feeling*, the *Gulbenkian Report: the Arts in Schools*, David Best's *Reason and Feeling in the Arts* – all share this conception. In fact, the very titles of the two authored volumes dramatize the insight.

One implication of this aesthetic for the curriculum is obvious: the arts must be conceived as one community. The arts belong together for they all work through the aesthetic modality and are preoccupied with the patterns of experience, particularly sentient experience, as they are formally reflected in the diverse symbols of art. The arts belong generically together and should be granted the same importance in the curriculum as other 'intellectual communities', such as the humanities and the sciences. This is the first general educational proposition of a conservationist aesthetic.

The second proposition derives more from the *conservationist* element and concerns an aesthetic awareness of the tradition. This actual reclamation of the various and neglected traditions of art – this restoration of the past tense in order to secure the proper aesthetic continuum of time is now under way. It can be seen in dance, for example, where Janet Adshead has begun a historic and analytic study of dance forms, thus making possible a sense of history where there has been only a sense of the contemporary. Drawing her work into educational dance, Anna Haynes has written about an expansion of dance education which would:

> include any kind of style of dance and an understanding of its form and purpose. Such an expansion frees dance from the confines of the contemporary. Here it has the potential to discover a new set of relationships and expressive possibilities within an historic continuum. Dance reconnects with its past and becomes potentially richer for the encounter. [12]

What Anna Haynes conceives of as the next development for dance is paradigmatic for most of the other arts. At the moment one can sense among many drama teachers a desire to connect with theatre, while English teachers cannot but be aware of the dynamic *Shakespeare in Schools Project* where Shakespeare is returning, in the most bodily and dramatic manner, to both primary and secondary classrooms. Indeed, even the traditional concepts of 'rhetoric' and 'poetics' are returning both to literary discourse and the practice of writing in the English lesson. These acts of conservation are all scattered signs of the new aesthetic.

Implications for the Visual Arts

I want now to narrow my attention to the visual arts.

In a critical paper published in *The Journal of Art and Design Education* in 1983 John Steers wrote:

> The greater part of the work of the art department is concerned with the production of art objects of one kind or another and little allowance is made for the development of critical aware-ness or an understanding of the cultural heritage of this country or of mankind as a whole. There is little obvious sequence in art education generally, or specifically in the secondary school. At every stage there is a tendency to ask pupils to start again at the

beginning and to ignore previous hard won experience ... (It is) a confused subject area generally lacking in direction and purpose.[13]

The diagnosis reveals nearly all the critical symptoms of Aesthetic Modernism as defined earlier in this chapter and in Chapter 5. For it was Modernism that insisted dogmatically that we 'start again at the beginning', from an impossible zero, from some assumed *tabula rasa* of the mind. Since 1983, though, there has been a formidable reaction against the 'tabula rasa classroom'. There has been a growing recognition that the child has to be brought into the visual culture, that he has to be made through the teaching of the arts a member of what Ernst Gombrich has called 'the cosmos of art'.[14] In this context the principal publication has been Rod Taylor's pioneering work *Education for Art*. This book, first published in 1986 and illustrated by the remarkable work of young students who had often gone unnoticed in the *tabula rasa* art-room, sought to show that one of the responsibilities of the art-teacher was precisely to 'promote critical awareness', 'an understanding of the cultural heritage of this country' and 'of mankind as a whole'. Taylor's book shows how all four elements of the aesthetic field – making, presenting, responding and evaluating (drawing on the

Plate 24   Martin Murray Reclining Nude *circa 1984. In British art one can locate an indigenous aesthetic rooted in the human figure and landscape.*

whole tradition) – can be brought in the right environment into a complex, interactive dance. The book can be seen to vindicate much of the theory and practice of a conservationist aesthetic.

This is not the place to demarcate (as we did for English studies in Chapter 3) the diverse genres of the visual arts. But it is of importance to my general ecological theme to consider further the renewal of interest in figurative and landscape art. Glancing over the rubble of International Modernism we find ourselves able to see, more clearly, certain continuities in British painting. As Peter Fuller has claimed:

> The best British artists have stubbornly maintained the traditions of an aesthetic rooted in the human figure and, indeed, in the imaginative and spiritual response to the whole world of natural form – including, of course, abstract forms derived from the experience of nature. [15]

Thus it is possible to discern powerful connections between Henry Moore, Graham Sutherland, Paul Nash and the great landscape tradition of the late eighteenth and nineteenth centuries: of Palmer, Cotman, Constable, Turner. The painter Paul Nash, in particular, was quite emphatic about the aesthetic siting of his own lyrical painting (and photography). He referred to the 'English idiom of painting' and saw that idiom as using 'a pronounced linear method in design, no doubt traceable to sources in Celtic ornament or the predilection for the Gothic idiom'. [16] Like so many of the landscape painters, his work is also central to our ecological understanding for it celebrates the fusion of imaginative consciousness and the organic structures of nature. It reveals a profound indwelling of mind within the order of nature.

Reflecting on this aspect of his work Herbert Read wrote:

> The natural organic fact, the present life of flower and leaf, invades the animistic landscape, the sacred habitation of familiar spirits. The shell, the fossil, the withered stalk, fungus, tree and cloud, are so many elements in a druidic ritual. The synthesis, the solution of the equation, is not literature: it is not metaphysics. It may be magic, but, if so, it is reviving the first and most potent function of art. [17]

Read's commentary comes close to understanding but then confuses with its talk of 'magic' and 'druidic rituals'. It might have been better to say that Nash perceptually discloses the creative life of consciousness-within-things. In his work (as in so much of the British figurative and landscape tradition) we contemplate the patterning of

175

nature as it is transformed through the imagination and the expressive qualities of paint. Nash's synthesis may be sacred but it is also, fundamentally, ecological – as, indeed, is the whole tradition to which the work belongs.

I mention the British landscape genre partly because it is one of the traditions which should be brought into the art classroom, but also because, once again, it demonstrates the necessary continuum between past and present and between consciousness and nature.

There are two further facets of a conservationist aesthetic which, in conclusion, I would like to briefly consider. The first, relates to the use of natural materials. The second, to the teaching of design.

For obvious reasons a conservationist aesthetic would be committed, but not exclusively so, to the use of natural materials. Seonaid Robertson has shown the value of natural dyes in fabric work, but she has been even more eloquent about the aesthetic potentiality of natural clay. In a recent interview she claimed:

> Clay has the special nature of plasticity. It will take the imprint of the youngest child, or the most accomplished potter. It seems almost to take the emotional imprint of each person; one can look at a model in clay and see what state of mind the person was in. A visit to a museum, or even handling one humble clay pot the teacher has brought in, comes alive when we try to identify with the maker, see his thumbprint.
>
> We can certainly show children that when they use clay they are part of a great tradition going back to the early history of mankind. Clay is the most indestructible of materials: when archaeologists dig into a site they often find the most information from pottery. And, looking forward to contemporary times, we can show children how great artists of today use clay for pottery and sculpture. Children can be led to feeling part of a living tradition. Clay is one of the important materials because of its wide location over the earth and its use from primitive times. I could teach every subject in the curriculum through clay.[18]

In her spontaneous remarks nearly all the central points of a conservationist aesthetic are quietly reiterated; using clay, she affirms, children feel they are part of a long tradition. As their fingers and hands make connection with the malleable clay so the clay connects them both to the earth and the variegated cultural forms of the past.

Finally, with regards to design, a conservationist aesthetic would make two fundamental points. The first is that design should be conceived as a specialized development coming out of a more comprehensive visual arts aesthetic. Only this could ensure that the concept of design (which is of the greatest importance) would be informed by a developed sense of beauty and unity. The practical tasks would then be met with *aesthetic intelligence*. In this connection we must not forget how modernist architecture failed because of its *unremitting functionalism*, isolating the technical problems from the environment, from the community, from the actual places where the buildings were sited, from the whole web of connections which define the human-cultural-natural continuum of our lives. It would be a tragedy, if having recently freed ourselves from the functional and monotonous forms of Late Modernism, their discredited utile premises were to be laid down for a vocational 'arts education' in this country. Demands for 'training', for 'skills,' in relationship to 'market forces' disconnected from meaning and from ecological understanding, must have disastrous consequences. Design will only be good when it comes out of a full aesthetic education and is a manifestation of that aesthetic intelligence which perceives holistically and is able to execute accordingly.

Conclusion

In this chapter I have argued that culture is natural, the aesthetic activity is the way in which the mind makes perceptual sense of the world and that it is formally developed through the arts. I have tried to show how, reacting against the exhaustion of Modernism, a conservationist aesthetic is at work in our culture and in our educational system, transforming our practices and expectations. I have suggested that this conservationism of mood has brought the arts together as a unified community and has engendered a radical commitment to tradition (seen as part of the aesthetic field). In particular, I have wanted to make explicit the connections between the symbols of art, the aesthetic intelligence which creates them and the formative energies of nature through which our aesthetic intelligence has evolved.

The arts are valuable partly because they reveal the lineaments of our own nature (within nature) to us. Among many other things, they can make us feel that here where we live is also where we belong. Significantly the word 'ecology' derives from the Greek word for *house*. The arts can often intensify and enhance that sense of belonging, of feeling that, for all the suffering and anguish, this planet is our home.

More than any other symbols, the symbols of art have the power to release and root that life-enhancing sense that: *in this vast structure I too belong and have my being.*

Notes

1. *Modern Painters* is a recent quarterly journal of the fine arts. It is edited by Peter Fuller and the first Spring issue was launched in February 1988.
2. See, particularly, *Aesthetics after Modernism* (Writers and Readers, 1982) and *Images of God* (Chatto and Windus, 1985). See also note 1.
3. See, particularly, *The Dilemma of Style* (John Murray, 1987).
4. See, for example, *The Aesthetics of Architecture* (Methuen, 1979) and *The Aesthetic Understanding* (Methuen, 1983).
5. D.W. Winnicott expressed this well when he wrote in *Playing and Reality* (Tavistock, 1971): 'It is not possible to be original except on the basis of tradition.'
6. MIDGLEY, M. (1979) *Beast and Man*, Harvester Press.
7. See *The Dilemma of Style, op cit.*
8. FRAMPTON, K. (1983) 'Towards a critical regionalism: Six points for an architecture of resistance', in *Post-Modern Culture*, (Pluto Press) p. 25.
9. HABERMAS, J. (1983) 'Modernity – an incomplete project' in *Post-Modern Culture*. I should point out that Habermas' *conclusions* are *not* the same as my own.
10. See POPPER, K. (1957) *The Poverty of Historicism*, Routledge and Kegan Paul. For its application to the Modernist Aesthetic see the opening chapter of ABBS, P. (Ed) *Living Powers: The Arts in Education*, Falmer Press.
11. See, for example, *The Study of Dance* (Dance Books Ltd, 1981) and *Dance History* (Dance Books Ltd, 1984).
12. HAYNES, A. (1987) 'Changing perspectives in dance education' in Abbs, P. (Ed) *Living Powers: The Arts in Education*, Falmer Press, p. 160.
13. STEERS, J. (1983) in *The Journal of Art and Design Education*.
14. GOMBRICH, E. (1984) *Tributes: Interpretations of Our Cultural History*, Phaidon.
15. Peter Fuller in editorial to the first edition of *Modern Painters* (Vol 1 No 1, spring 1988).
16. READ, H. (1944) *Paul Nash*, Penguin Books, p. 16
17. *Ibid.*
18. ROBERTSON, S. (1987) *The Studio Potter*, 15, 2, June. See also ROBERTSON, S. (1982) *Rosegarden and Labyrinth: A Study in Art Education*, Gryphon Press.

Bibliographies

Arts and Education

ABBS, P. (1975) *Reclamations: Essays on Culture, Mass Culture and the Curriculum*, Gryphon Press.

ABBS, P. (Ed.) (1987) *Living Powers: The Arts in Education*, Falmer Press.

ASPIN, D. (1984) *Objectivity and Assessment in the Arts: The Problem of Aesthetic Education*, NAEA.

BANTOCK, G.M. (1967) *Education, Culture and the Emotions*, Faber and Faber.

BERLEANT, A. (1970) *The Aesthetic Field*, Charles C. Thomas.

BEST, D. (1985) *Feeling and Reason in the Arts*, Allen and Unwin.

BLOOMFIELD, A. (Ed) *Creative and Aesthetic Education Aspects*, 34, University of Hull.

BROUDY, H (1972) *Enlightened Cherishing: An Essay in Aesthetic Education*, University of Illinois Press.

CASSIRER, E. (1944) *An Essay on Man*, Bantam Books.

CASSIRER, E. (1955–8) *The Philosophy of Symbolic Forms* (in three volumes), Yale University Press.

COLLINGWOOD, R. G. (1958) *The Principles of Art*, Oxford University Press

DEWEY, J. (1934) *Art as Experience*, Minton Balch and Company.

DONOGHUE, D. (1985) *The Arts Without Mystery*, BBC.

EAGLETON, T. (1983) *Literary Theory*, Basil Blackwell.

ELIOT, T.S. (1975) *Selected Prose of TS Eliot*, edited Frank Kermode, Faber and Faber.

FREUD, S. (1973a) *Introductory Lectures on Psychoanalysis*, Penguin.

FREUD, S. (1973b) *New Introductory Lectures on Psychoanalysis*, Penguin.

FRYE, N. (1957) *The Anatomy of Criticism*, Princeton University Press.

FULLER, P. (1980a) *Art and Psycho-Analysis*, Writers and Readers.

FULLER, P. (1980b) *Beyond the Crisis in Art*, Writers and Readers.

FULLER, P. (1982) *Aesthetics after Modernism*, Writers and Readers.

FULLER, P. (1985) *Images of God*, Chatto and Windus.

GOMBRICH, E. (1960) *Art and Illusion*, Phaidon.

GOMBRICH, E. (1966) *Norm and Form*, Phaidon.

GOMBRICH, E. (1979) *The Sense of Order*, Phaidon.

GOMBRICH, E. (1978) *The Story of Art*, Phaidon.

GOMBRICH, E. (1984) *Tributes: Interpreters of our Cultural Tradition*, Phaidon.

GULBENKIAN FOUNDATION (1982) *The Arts in Schools*, Gulbenkian Foundation.
HARGREAVES, D. (1982) *The Challenge of the Comprehensive School*, Routledge and Kegan Paul.
HOSPERS, J. (1969) *Introductory Readings in Aesthetics*, Collier MacMillan.
JONES, D. (1973) *Epoch and Artist*, Faber and Faber.
JUNG, C. *et al* (1964) *Man and his Symbols*, Aldus Books.
JUNG, C. (1967) *The Spirit in Man, Art and Literature*, Routledge and Kegan Paul.
KANT, I. (1952a) *Critique of Pure Reason*, Oxford University Press.
KANT, I. (1952b) *Critique of Judgement*, Oxford University Press.
KOESTLER, A. (1975) *The Act of Creation*, Picador.
LANGER, S. (1953) *Feeling and Form*, Routledge and Kegan Paul.
LANGER, S. (1957a) *Philosophy in a New Key*, Havard University Press.
LANGER, S. (1957b) *Problems of Art*, Routledge and Kegan Paul.
LANGER, S. (1974) *Mind: An Essay on Human Feeling*, Johns Hopkins University Press.
LIPMAN, M. (Ed) (1973) *Contemporary Aesthetics*, Allyn and Bacon.
LODGE, D. (1981) *Working with Structuralism*, Routledge and Kegan Paul.
MARCUSE, H. (1978) *The Aesthetic Dimension*, Macmillan.
MORDAUNT CROOK, J. (1987) *The Dilemma of Style*, John Murray.
MUMFORD, L. (1971) *The Myth of the Machine*, Secker and Warburg.
PHENIX, P. (1964) *Realms of Meaning*, McGraw Hill.
POLANYI, M. (1973) *Personal Knowledge*, Routledge and Kegan Paul.
READ, H. (1943) *Education through Art*, Faber and Faber.
READ, H. (1955) *Ikon and Idea*, Faber and Faber.
REDFERN, H.B. (1986) *Questions in Aesthetic Education*, Allen and Unwin.
REID, L.A. (1961) *Ways of Knowledge and Experience*, Allen and Unwin.
REID, L.A. (1970) *Meaning in the Arts*, Allen and Unwin.
REID, L.A. (1986) *Ways of Understanding and Education*, Heinemann Educational Books.
ROBERTSON, S. (1982) *Rosegarden and Labyrinth: Art in Education*, Gryphon Press.
ROSS, M. (1975) *Arts and the Adolescent*, Schools Council, Evans.
ROSS, M. (1978) *The Creative Arts*, Heinemann Educational Books.
ROSS, M. (Ed) (1983) *The Arts in Education*, Falmer Press.
ROSS, M. (1984) *The Aesthetic Impulse*, Pergamon.
SCHILLER (1974) *On the Aesthetic Education of Man*, Clarendon Press.
SCRUTON, R. (1974) *Art and Imagination*, Methuen.
SCRUTON, R. (1979) *The Aesthetics of Architecture*, Methuen.
SCRUTON, R. (1983) *The Aesthetic Understanding*, Metheun.
STEINER, G. (1967) *Language and Silence*, Penguin.
STEINER G. (1986) *Real Presences*, Cambridge University Press.
STOKES, A. (1965) *The Invitation in Art*, Tavistock.
STORR, A. (1972) *Dynamics of Creation*, Penguin.
TIPPETT, M. (1974) *Moving Into Aquarius*, Picador.
VALERY, P. (1964) *Aesthetics*, Routledge and Kegan Paul.
WARNOCK, M. (1980) *Imagination*, Faber and Faber.

WHALLEY, G. (1953) *Poetic Process* Greenwood Press.
WINNICOT, D.W. (1971) *Playing and Reality*, Tavistock.
WITKIN, R. (1974) *The Intelligence of Feeling*, Heinemann Educational Books.
WITTGENSTEIN, L. (1966) *Lectures and Conversations on Aesthetics, Psychology and Religious Belief*, Oxford University Press.
WOLLHEIM, R. (1970) *Art and its Objects: An Introduction to Aesthetics*, Harper and Row.

English

ABBS, P. (1976) *Root and Blossom*, Heinemann.
ABBS, P. (1982) *English Within the Arts*, Hodder and Stoughton.
ALLEN, D. (1980) *English Teaching Since 1965*, Heinemann Educational Books.
BARNES, D. (1969) *From Communication to Curriculum*, Penguin.
BARNES, D. and TODD, (1969) *Language, the Learner and the School*, Penguin.
BRITTON, J. (1972) *Language and Learning*, Penguin.
COOK, C. (1917) *The Play Way*, Heinemann.
CREBER, J. (1965) *Sense and Sensitivity*, University of London Press.
DIXON, J. (1975) *Growth through English*, Oxford University Press.
HARRISON, B. (1982) *An Arts-based Approach to English*, Hodder and Stoughton.
HOLBROOK, D. (1961) *English for Maturity*, Cambridge University Press.
HOLBROOK, D. (1979) *English for Meaning*, NFER.
HOURD, M. (1949) *The Education of the Poetic Spirit*, Heinemann Educational Books.
ROSENBLATT, L. (1970) *Literature as Exploration*, Heinemann Educational Books.
SAMPSON, G. (1975) *English for the English*, Cambridge University Press.
SCHAYER, D. (1972) *The Teaching of English in Schools 1900–1970*, Routledge and Kegan Paul.
WHITEHEAD, F. (1971) *The Disappearing Dais*, Chatto and Windus.
WILKINSON, A. (1971) *The Foundations of Language*, Oxford University Press.

Autobiography and Education

ABBS, P.F. (1974) *Autobiography in Education*, Gryphon Press.
BOTTRALL, M. (1958) *Everyman a Pheonix: Studies in Seventeenth Century Autobiography*, John Murray.
BUCKLEY, J.H. (1984) *The Turning Key*, Harvard University Press.
DELANY, P. (1969) *British Autobiography in the Seventeenth Century*, Routledge and Kegan Paul.
EGAN, S. (1984) *Patterns of Experience in Autobiography*, University of North Carolina Press.
FLEISHMAN, A. (1983) *Figures of Autobiography*, University of North Carolina Press.
JAY, P. (1984) *Being in the Text: Self Expression from Wordsworth to Roland Barthes*, Cornell University Press.

JELINEK E. (Ed) (1980) *Women's Autobiography*, Indiana University Press.

MISCH, G. (1973) *A History of Autobiography in Antiquity*, Vols 1 & 2, Greenwood Press.

MORRIS, J. (1966) *Versions of the Self*, Basic Books.

OLNEY, J. (1972) *Metaphors of Self – The Meaning of Autobiography*, Princeton University Press.

OLNEY, J. (Ed) (1980) *Autobiography: Essays Theoretical and Critical*, Princeton University Press.

PAOLINI, S. (1982) *Confessions of Sin and Love in the Middle Ages*, University Press of America

PASCAL, R. (1960) *Design and Truth in Autobiography*, Routledge and Kegan Paul.

PATEMAN, T. (1960) *Autobiography and Education*, Occasional Paper No 13, Education Area, University of Sussex.

PATERSON, L. (1986) *Victorian Autobiography: The Tradition of Self Interpretation*, Oxford University.

PILLING, J. (1981) *Autobiography and Imagination – Studies in Self-Scrutiny*, Routledge and Kegan Paul.

SHUMAKER, W. (1954) *English Autobiography: Its Emergence, Materials and Forms*, University of California Press.

SPENGEMANN, W.C. (1980) *The Forms of Autobiography: Episodes in the History of a Genre*, Yale University Press.

STARR, G.A. (1965) *Defoe and Spiritual Autobiography*, Princeton University Press.

STONE, A.E. (Ed) (1981) *The American Autobiography – a Collection of Critical Essays*, Prentice Hall.

TRILLING, L. (1972) *Sincerity and Authenticity*, Oxford University Press.

VINCENT, D. (1982) *Bread, Knowledge and Freedom: A Study of Nineteenth Century Working Class Autobiography*, Methuen.

WEINTRAUB, K. (1978) *The Value of the Individual: Self Circumstance and Autobiography*, University of Chicago Press.

Index